DEPUTY

Know Your Rights

A Cop's True Stories

by

Alfred Anderson

Deputy: Know Your Rights
A Cop's True Stories

© 2023 Alfred Anderson
a.anderson@accomn.com

Author: Alfred Anderson

Cover Design: Liam Beale

Layout Design: Richard Powell

Editing, Proofreading: Carol Ferias

Self-Publishing Consulting:
Digital Authors LLC, www.digital-authors.com

Contents

Foreword

In writing this book it was my intention to provide the reader an inside look at the life of a Deputy Sheriff, or for that matter, any Law Enforcement Officer (LEO). This text goes through the process of becoming one and living as one. It includes many anecdotal stories, some very sobering and others humorous. My desire is to inform the reader that most LEOs are not enemies of the citizenry but rather friends and neighbors. I speak for myself but I'm sure most Deputies feel the same way. We are and should be servants to the people who elected our boss, the Sheriff. The citizens of the county vote for the Sheriff to enforce the law and keep the community safe, but also to protect their rights.

I will cover much of that concept throughout the book and hope that I educate the reader about something that most know little; their constitutional rights. The state of American education is abysmal! And that is not hyperbole. I know of no local K–12 education system in the U.S.A. that teaches specifically courses on the Constitution and the Bill of Rights; courses that thoroughly explain the origins and rights that every citizen is endowed with by our Creator. Our Founding Fathers knew what they were doing.

This book is dual-purposed in that I present my experiences but also explain the use of our rights. So it is my hope that the reader finds what I have written in this book engaging, interesting and informative. It is my desire that the reader will not put the book down because, in their mind, it doesn't flow well or is boring. I want the reader's eyes to be opened and I want them to maybe laugh along the way. So, please enjoy.

Chapter 1
911 Hangup

A 911 hangup call is always of great urgency and trepidation for a Law Enforcement Officer. I am Deputy Anderson, with a rural northern county in Idaho. I have just completed my ten hour swing shift this night and am at home removing all of my gear when I get a call at 3:00 am. Our department, The Mountain County Sheriff's Department, does not have a large contingency of Patrol Officers, and during the swing shift in its early morning hours there is usually just one Patrol Deputy on duty. Our county is large, with 3800 square miles of mountains, federal forests, and various small towns. A Deputy has to cover a lot of miles in one day.

The call comes in from our Dispatch Department located in the county seat of Buffalo. Laurie, the Dispatcher, says that they just received a 911 call that disconnected right away. "No one spoke, no noise in the background, just hung up," she says.

"Ok," I reply, "give me the location." With such calls, most dispatch centers are able to trace the call to the exact location; ours is no different. I know now that my night has just gotten longer.

With these kinds of calls, there is always a rush of adrenaline as one prepares to go and find out what is occurring. Immediately I redress myself with a pair of jeans, uniform top, and all of my gear. For those that have never worn a badge, "all of my gear" is a lot of stuff. A bullet proof vest, sidearm, duty belt with two extra pistol magazines, two sets of handcuffs, pepper spray, collapsible baton, and handheld radio with the mic hooked to my left epaulet are what we wear; that's minimal, for in our future we will have a taser and audio video camera hanging on us, and maybe more. After five minutes of preparation, I am out the door.

I hop into my patrol car, a Ford Explorer, also known as "Exploder" by the force, and am on my way, 30 miles south of my home. This situation normally calls for a "Code 3" run, lights and siren, but because it is 3:30 am, I use the siren sparingly with my overhead lights flashing. With very little traffic in the largest town of Payette, I quickly reach its outskirts, where I can really put "the pedal to the metal".

The life of a Law Enforcement Officer in rural Idaho is one of poor pay, long hours, and routine. Ninety percent of our time is spent with routine work. The common refrain for a Law Enforcement Officer (LEO) is, "90% boredom punctuated by 10% sheer terror." To some degree, I would agree with that.

Anyway, most people enter law enforcement and fire

fighting for the very thing I am going through at the moment. The thrill of running a patrol unit at high speed in front of onlookers is always exhilarating. Some become "junkies" doing it and can't leave the profession. For me it is always a thrill as well, but I think I have better control of my emotions regarding it. I got into law enforcement late after years of working as a "civilian".

My thoughts at the moment are of wondering what happened at the location where I am going. There are several horrible possibilities that cross my mind and I know I am facing it alone, no backup. In a sparsely-populated county, one does not have the luxury of numerous other officers or agencies available. Sometimes we simply have to go in alone. Commonly, such dispatch calls are a result of domestic abuse, and a spouse, most likely female, has tried to get help but is stopped by the aggressive partner. This is never good and our training says "don't go in alone." The danger is too great with just one officer involved and bloodshed could result. Another scenario is a person is reaching out for help because life has become meaningless and they want it to end. With both situations I am rushing toward disaster.

The lights along the highway are speeding by quickly as I approach a small village. I have another ten miles to go and my mind is ruminating over the help I will need. What will I find? As a Law Enforcement Officer, one must be prepared to face one of the many unusual and potentially dangerous madnesses that humans perpetrate on others. Training demands that we expect the unexpected and face it with as much reason and calmness that can be mustered under such circumstances. It's rare that the civilian will face such things in their normal daily life, but with us "civil servants," that 10% of sheer terror can rear its ugly head at any moment. It's the profession we have chosen.

It doesn't take long to arrive at the scene, and I am in a vacant rural area surrounded by trees and have come to a dirt path leading to a lone, single wide trailer home. It's dark, very dark, with only a few distant security lights shining around me. I call Dispatch to let them know that I have arrived at the location and would be out with portable radio contact. My Code 3 run was terminated about two miles back so as to not alert the "bad guys" if any. My patrol unit is left back and somewhat out of sight of the home, and I begin to walk slowly and quietly down the grassy pathway. My side arm, a Glock 22, is out with a hollow point .40 caliber bullet chambered as it always is when I'm on duty. When one has to "cock" the gun, pull the slide back to insert a round in the chamber, that split second could cost an officer his life. Time is everything in a gunfight. Action versus reaction has about a minimum of .75 seconds between the two.

With my flashlight in hand, I am nearing the outside deck of the home. It is quiet, with no lights emanating from within and my thoughts begin to suspect suicide. I begin thinking of the time when another Deputy and I investigated a reported suicide. That was during the daylight hours and there were two of us. When we entered the house we found an older woman seated in a Lazy Boy chair with a small hole in her forehead. She had ended her pain-ridden life of cancer with a .22 bullet.

Putting those thoughts aside, I knock on the door and call out, "Sheriff's Department." No answer from within. Once again, "Sheriff's Department, anyone inside?" Again there is silence. *Well*, I am thinking, *here I go,* and know that I must do a room to room search. The door is unlocked, *uh-oh*, so I enter, cautiously, with my gun in my right hand and flashlight in my left tucked up next to the gun and outward from my body. That way, if someone hiding inside wants to shoot me, they are most likely going to shoot at the light and miss my body, which is protected with a bulletproof vest.

The entry point is the living room and as I scan left to right, I see nothing threatening, just the normal coach, chairs and television. My eyes are moving everywhere to see if any movement catches their attention. I can feel my heart beating in my chest and my breathing is fast. I know adrenaline is pumping into my system and I need to calm down, if possible. I consciously slow my breathing and continue to look, listen, and smell. Smell is an important sense, for it can reveal drug chemicals, alcoholic drinks, and death. The smell of death and blood is distinct and can alert one to danger.

I advance to the kitchen and see nothing. Next is the long hallway leading to two bedrooms and a bathroom. Suicide is now the more probable event, and those are never pretty. Having experienced them, they can be downright ugly and messy, and seeing them alone in the middle of the night can be like seeing a bad, or good, depending on one's perspective, horror flick in real life.

Man, what am I doing here at 42 years of age and a daughter at home, I think. The hairs on my neck are standing out as I proceed to the first bedroom all the while still calling out, "Sheriff's Department."

The door to the bedroom is open and I swing quickly into the room with my gun pointed to any potential target. A Deputy cannot leave any space unchecked; not even under the bed or in the closet. Danger can lurk anywhere. Even false walls in larger homes can hide evil. In a mobile home like this one, though, that is not likely.

With the first bedroom cleared, the place I fear most is next; the bathroom, and of course, its door is closed. With thoughts of blood everywhere, I open the door and notice that the tub/shower is behind the door. I shine my light into the mirror to possibly get a brief glimpse and blunt the effect of what I might see.

That's an illusion! A mirror will still show the full bloodiness and gore of a shotgun blast, maybe not in its entirety but still horrible.

Whew, the bathroom reveals no bad news. Suddenly I find myself breathing again. I quickly scan the rest of the bathroom and back out with my eye on the bedroom.

Surprisingly, I find myself relaxing a bit with the bathroom past. I move onto the back bedroom, which is open. I repeat the same scan and find nothing again.

I am jolted out of my intenseness by a call from Dispatch; "2114, what is your status?"

I tell them I am Code 4, (ok) and have just completed the home search with negative findings. "Will proceed to check exterior" I say.

"10-4" they reply.

I am thinking, *Why was the front door open and only the bathroom door closed?* It's as though the devil himself is playing with me and I quickly put those thoughts aside because I still have more to do. Outside could hide the real danger with my going inside being the trap. This is not perverse thinking; my officer training dictates that I don't take anything for granted because an officer in uniform is always a target, and even out of uniform, too. That's why I and most officers carry a weapon all the time. Too many have been surveilled and ambushed while off duty, even at home. That is a sad commentary of life in the United States and most of the world for Law Enforcement Officers. The common refrain, "Once an officer, always an officer" is so true.

As I leave to go back outside, I look up to see the brilliant star-lit night. It is peaceful and quiet and I hear the distant yip of a coyote. I think how sad it is that I live in such a beautiful part of the world of majestic mountains, thick pine forests, ambling rivers, and a myriad of wildlife, and yet it can harbor such ugliness of human evil.

I jerk my mind back into drive and focus on the unfinished job, what potentially lurks outside. Mobile homes are by design up off the ground with some sort of skirting around the base. With the same method used inside, my gun is pointed ahead with the flashlight beside it. I cautiously walk down the two steps that lead from the deck and inspect below it. Although I pretty much feel that my job is finished and all was a false alarm, I remain attentive to any possible threat that could be hiding underneath. It's not the time to become complacent. Slowly, I continue around the perimeter of the house looking for openings in the skirting, but see none. My flashlight is the only illumination that guides my vision. There is no security light that would otherwise illuminate the outside. It's as if no one has ever lived here.

Finally, I am done. As what happens too often, it is another false alarm, and I report back to Dispatch that conclusion, and that I am ok. I inform them that I will be heading back to the "barn".

My body aches from all of the adrenaline that was injecting into my body. I feel it especially around my ribs. Adrenaline is a good thing when facing danger. Flight or fight are the options when humans face danger, but regardless, it has its negative effect on the body.

I climb into my patrol unit and begin the ride back to my home, some 30 miles away. I live in the northern part of this expansive county, which includes a large federal wilderness region only accessible by non-motorized vehicles. I and my fellow Deputies have to travel long distances to get from one end to the other and at each end are dangerous winding canyons.

As I drive through the small village I passed earlier, on the outskirts is a clump of willows and brush. Suddenly, I see a large bull elk moving along the edge of the road of that patch, and I slow down to admire his antlers and size. It brings a smile to my face to know that I am so lucky to see more of the beauty that Mountain County has to offer.

When I reach my home, I park the Explorer in my garage and walk into the peace and calmness that familiar safe surroundings offer. It is now nearly 6:00 am and it's time to awaken my daughter Lindsay to get ready for school. She is pretty self-sufficient and I trust her to get ready and make her own breakfast. She will drive our old Suburban to the high school in Payette where she is a junior.

As for me, I shed all of my gear and clothes and put on my sleeping shorts and t-shirt. As soon as I inform her, I let her know that I stayed out late and promise to fill her in later. I tell her to be safe and have a good day, before I finally lay down to try and entice sleep to come, but this morning sleep would come slowly.

Chapter 2
Changing Directions

Most people enter the profession at a young age, normally in their early twenties. I was a latecomer after years of owning and running small businesses. My expertise was in selling people on the products I offered in my businesses. I mention this because, as I will explain later, it was a very important ability to have. I had several years prior been divorced and had been diagnosed with Type 1 Diabetes.

I know the week that it happened as I was visiting a friend in Chandler, Arizona, on the third week of January, 1993. Arizona is a naturally dry climate and one gets thirsty. So I was drinking a lot of Pepsi but also urinating a lot. I just thought the latter was a result of the former. Drink a lot, pee a lot. Well, I returned back home to Park Rapids, Minnesota and that night my three good friends and I were scheduled to have our weekly card games of Hearts, for money, of course. The pattern of drinking and peeing continued and I mentioned it to my good friend, Paul, a veterinarian.

After hearing my commentary about excessive thirst and urination, he unequivocally stated that I must be diabetic.

"No," I exclaimed, "that can't be. This is just a problem of drinking too much pop and beer. Nothing more, I'm healthy." Denial is a powerful elixir for things we fear facing. However, my mind and logic were telling me something different.

Paul said, "I'll bring a test strip for you to pee on when I come over tonight. We'll see."

My mind was suddenly racing with thoughts of my grandfather Alfred, who had the same disease. He developed it at about the same age, and I had heard that the disease skipped generations. With no one else in the family of his progeny with the disease, I would be the first. That figures. I was named after him and he died two months before I was born; hence I was given his name.

So Paul brought the strip, I peed on it, and sure enough, it indicated that my urine was full of sugar and I was suffering from Diabetes Melitus.

Now, there are two forms of this disease: Type 1 and Type 2. Type 1 is often called Juvenile Diabetes since most of the time it starts when a person is young, although not always. Type 2 is more typical for people of my age where one is overweight, lacking in exercise, and has a generally bad diet. I didn't really fit those parameters. My weight was reasonable, I exercised a fair amount, and had a good diet.

So, what happened? Dr. Johnson, my physician, originally

diagnosed me as Type 2 and put me on a medication that would help my body utilize the insulin I produced better. This is the common remedy for folks with later life diabetic symptoms. Type 2 diabetics produce insulin but their bodies aren't accepting it well, and the medication corrects that.

I was working at the time as a field technician/salesman for a chemical company and traveling a lot around the Dakotas and Minnesota. I am/was a pilot and flew on occasion in my Money 231 airplane. The one thing about diabetes is that one would not be permitted to pilot an aircraft solo. Because of possible blackouts associated with low blood sugar, similar to individuals who have had heart attacks, it is just too dangerous to issue a flight medical to such a person.

Being that I wasn't officially designated as that severe a risk with Type 2, I continued to fly. However, the sword of Damocles dropped on me after several months of losing weight, some 50 pounds, and experiencing raging thirst and urination. The need to pee was so strong at times that I had to stop the car and do so along the road, or urinate in a container I kept in the car.

I finally went back to see my doctor to tell him the maladies I was experiencing. He saw the emaciated look on my face and the loss of weight and immediately told me that I had to go to insulin injections or I would die. He was actually surprised that I had let it go that far.

I told him, "Look, Doc, I'll lose my flight medical certificate and won't be able to fly anymore; it's my life!"

He, without hesitation said, "You have already lost it and I won't renew it, and if you don't do something immediately you could die at any moment. Period."

I asked, "What happened to me? What caused this? I kind of know the week that it started, but it was so sudden."

He answered, "Knowing your genetic history with your grandfather, I believe you were infected with a virus similar to polio called the Coxsackie virus, and your immune system attacked it as well as your Islets of Langerhans Beta cells located in your pancreas, which produce insulin."

I asked, "Why were the Beta cells attacked as well?"

He said that the enzymes associated with both the virus and Beta cells are very similar and my immune system attacked both. "Those appear to have been destroyed and you no longer produce insulin. It is called an autoimmune attack."

My mind was swirling and my heart pounding in my chest for what I now faced. No longer could I fly and I was facing the rest of my life poking myself with sharp needles. What the hell kind of life would that be?

I'm normally a pretty tough guy mentally. I don't get depressed, but boy was I about to test that characteristic. Doubts, despair, and sadness would plague my thinking, and I knew I had to "buck up" or lose it. My life was about to take a dramatic turn.

First, I had to resolve to survive and live a normal, healthy life. That meant not just accepting my condition, but embracing it. I don't mean that it in a loving type of embrace, but in one that is a fight of an ugly beast called Diabetes. So I worked with Doc Johnson to learn as much as I could about the disease and how to best manage it. That meant testing my blood often with a personal diabetic meter and test strips to know what level my blood sugar was and to compensate with the amount of insulin to use to keep those levels normal. He stressed that I could live a perfectly normal life with this regimen, but I was the arbiter of my own fate. No one else would or could do that for me.

Ok, I thought, *if that is what must be done, that is what I will do.* I truly say "thank God" for the modern technology that we have now to overcome a disease that in the past was really a debilitating one and a destroyer of the human body. My grandfather never had that luxury. It was purely a guessing game at that time.

I add that, now, as I write this, the advent of even more advanced technology such as wearable insulin pumps and continuous glucose sensors in the body has made control a breeze.

It hasn't been easy. I remember often when my blood glucose went low, hypoglycemic, and my mental functions wouldn't work or I passed out.

People would ask, "What's wrong with Alfred?"

My brothers could recite many stories of such incidents and say, "He needs some orange juice."

The close people around me knew the indicators well and would lovingly respond. My good friend Paul would kid me and say "I like it when you are low, I can beat you at cribbage." He is an opportunistic asshole. We played for a dollar a win and a dime for every point back. He took my money with glee.

Anyway, it was never easy exactly calculating the necessary insulin to dose myself with and it was hard to recognize when I was going low.

That is why the FAA would not let me fly. I had moved to Story, Wyoming and flew between the Park Rapids, Minnesota, and the Buffalo, Wyoming airports. The change of residency to Wyoming from Minnesota saved me a lot of money in taxes; enough that I could pay for the house I bought there. The move took me from one of the highest taxed states to the lowest in the lower 48. That justified my move and I was still able to work by flying to where I worked. What would take 13 hours by car took only three hours in my Mooney 231, a turbo-charged retractable four-passenger plane that flew at 200+ miles per hour. Interestingly, the route took me directly over Devils Tower.

The remainder of that year was a struggle to find balance. I was traveling a lot for my company and it just wasn't working out. I lost heart to continue and at the end of the year I resigned my position. I began the dropout phase of my life.

From Wyoming I decided to drive my '84 diesel Suburban to Key Largo, Florida and just hang out.

So began my long trek to a law enforcement career. Once I arrived in Florida, I bought a 29-foot Free Spirit Holiday Rambler travel trailer, kind of an apropos name for my new home. I rented a space along Overseas Highway 1 that goes all the way to the end of the keys to Key West. I and my miniature Schnauzer, Shelby, settled down to spend the winter of '94 in paradise. Well, maybe not so much.

After a couple of days of sitting around, exploring, and experiencing life in the Keys, I decided I needed something to do. So, I got two part-time jobs working at the local Arby's and Pizza Hut. I chose those because I loved the food. If I like it so much, I might as well learn how to make it. I could tell many stories about working in those two places, but that is for another time.

So, what was it that triggered my mind to explore being a Law Enforcement Officer?

Well, the Arby's restaurant was located on the main highway between a Publix supermarket and a very poor district of black and Haitian people. I knew it was not really a safe zone and I kept a weapon in my vehicle. One day, a Publix employee came rushing into the Arby's to say his partner was wrestling with a shoplifter outside in the parking lot and he needed to call the Sheriff.

I told him to use the phone where I was working and then went outside to see what was happening. With a large package at their feet, I saw the Publix employee struggling with the thief.

I proceeded to insert myself into the scuffle and I told the guy, "Let me do this, I can handle him." I grabbed the scumbag around his neck, grasped his arm, and with one quick swipe of my leg, judo-style, he went down onto the asphalt.

Oh, I thought, *that probably hurt,* as he face-planted with a hard thud on the asphalt with an expulsion of air. I convinced him to cooperate. I kept my knee on his back until the Monroe County Sheriff Deputy arrived shortly thereafter.

The Publix guy exclaimed "Wow, that was cool. How did you do that so quickly and easily?"

I said, "Judo, my man, simple leverage." Of course after making a report to the Deputy and returning to work, I began to think that yeah, that was cool and kind of fun. It made me feel good.

One more incident at this restaurant cemented my desire to pursue something in law. I began to think about looking into becoming a lawyer or Law Enforcement Officer. I checked out the University of Wyoming Law School in Laramie on what it would take for further education to become a lawyer; I already had a degree from a college in England after going first to the University of Colorado to study engineering.

I discovered it would take another three years at the

University of Wyoming to accomplish it. I also investigated becoming a Cop, Constable on Patrol, a term from England.

Thinking about all of this, I was working one night at the Arby's around 7 pm. One of the girls that worked there was an attractive young black woman. We got along pretty well, even though she questioned me once on why I was working there. She said, "You're too smart and fancy pants to be working here. What are you doing here?"

So I explained my reasons and she accepted them. So, with that considered, I was working in the back, cleaning things up when all of a sudden another young male Haitian employee came rushing back to where I was, grabbed two big butcher knives, and turned on a big black male coming in after him who was shouting, "I'm going to kill you, motherfucker."

Without hesitation, crazy me jumped in between them with arms outstretched and shouted "Stop! What the hell is going on?"

The big guy spit out, "That motherfucker is messing with my girl."

I told them both to take it outside before we had bloodshed. The boyfriend left and the Haitian put the knives down.

The thundercloud passed for now until another was soon to come. Evidently, according to his girlfriend, the Haitian kid patted her on the behind and made some unsavory comments. It didn't take long for that to get back to the boyfriend. By the size and look of him, I wouldn't want to piss him off, either.

We continued our normal chores of closing the store. All seemed to have calmed down when suddenly the boyfriend was back, only this time with an Uzi submachine gun. He was pointing it over the glass partitions of the front counter, screaming he was going to shoot the motherfucker that touched his woman.

My survival mode kicked in and I, the only white face in the store, wasn't going to stick around to see the finale to this mess. Out the back door I ran to my car, grabbed my gun, and waited for the sound of gunfire. I was sure I would hear the buzz of that Uzi suddenly spit death. If the boyfriend came back out after shooting and possibly killing several, he would be in my sights. I wasn't going to let him go free, no warning, just shoot him.

However, the gunfire never came, and I began to hear sirens coming our way. I later learned that Rhonda, his girlfriend, stopped him from doing anything and he escaped out another door. It was explained to me later that the boyfriend was a felon and was wanted for murder in Ohio. His access to such a restricted weapon was not a surprise. Criminals will always have access to guns. Laws only take them from the good people.

The Monroe County Deputies arrived in force and took control of the situation quickly. However, it didn't last long, since both participants in the fight had disappeared and only us few employees answered their inquiries.

Not much to say. Rhonda had taken control and got her sorry ass boyfriend the hell out of the way.

I never knew if they found him or not, only that from then on I wasn't going to stick around this area much longer. It was time for me to head back home, but with the desire to explore what law enforcement was all about. The few short weeks I had left in Florida I took the LSAT (Law Scholastic Aptitude Test), a test for students that want to enter law school, and although I did ok, it was just too late in the year to apply for the Law School at the University of Wyoming in Laramie or any other university, for that matter.

Somewhat disappointed, I pondered on what to do. I had a good friend living in Twin Falls, Idaho, whom I had trained to take over the job that I had left. He mentioned that there was a college there that offered a law enforcement curriculum. I asked him to check it out. He got back to me quickly with the information to apply and said there was availability for the upcoming fall session.

So I applied, got accepted, and began my transition from Wyoming to Idaho to attend the College of Southern Idaho.

Oh boy, here I was almost 41-years-old, handicapped with a fickle disease and wondering how this was all about to play out.

Was I physically fit enough to handle this career? Could I control the diabetes sufficiently so as not to hinder me?

Mentally I was ready to embark on something new. I had some experience previously while attending a college in

England working as a security guard, and I liked it. I am not an office person, so I realized that being a lawyer was not for me. I liked working outdoors and being a Law Enforcement Officer was probably the way to travel that path. So, in the fall of '94, I began a new adventure.

Chapter 3
Learning Law

After selling my home in Wyoming, and pretty much everything else, I moved my travel trailer to Twin Falls and began the year-long course of P.O.S.T. (Police Officer Standards & Training) for the state of Idaho. After nearly 20 years of being out of the education lifestyle, going back into it was a bit strange but also exhilarating. Learning something new was always fun and of great interest for me, and walking around a small community college grounds as a middle-aged man surrounded by teenagers and early 20-year-olds seemed a bit out of place to me. But, oh well, here I was about to embark on an adventure that would be one of the best and most eye-opening of my life.

I enrolled in the year-long Law Enforcement curriculum which would result in an A.A.S. (Associates of Applied Sciences) degree but also a P.O.S.T. certification, which qualified me to be hired as a full-fledged Law Enforcement Officer in the state of Idaho. Each state has its own certification process, but they are all pretty similar. When one wants to recertify in another state, the process is much shorter, usually just involving learning the new set of laws for that state.

There were only 12 of us in that year's class. All the other students were pretty young, between 18 and 20. They were a disparate group of individuals: physically, personality, character, and education. They pretty much reflected society as a whole.

I would like to say that just because someone desires to be a police officer doesn't mean their character will change. They bring to the profession all of their positives and negatives. Unfortunately, we have seen in many news stories about cops, too many of the negatives. Although ethics training was a big part of our education, it doesn't always inculcate into the hearts and minds of young people. I had a big advantage in that phase of training. I actually believed strongly in the ideals of righteous and moral policing. I lived by the adage that "Humility is the catalyst that makes power benevolent."

After years of getting kicked and beaten down for my own stupid behavior, I entered the program with a level of humility that young people rarely have. I was quickly named "Grandpa" by my fellow classmates. It was an affectionate moniker mostly that sometimes crossed over to ridicule. But it was all in fun. More on humility and power later.

Our curriculum involved many subjects: ethics, constitutional law, state law, physical training, officer safety, weapons training, first aid, and much more. Our lead professor, Frank Dobbs, was in his fifties and a retired

Law Enforcement Officer. He was an excellent teacher. His experience and humor lent great credibility to what he presented. I personally liked him a lot. When I first interviewed with him for the course, he didn't feel that my age would be a problem. Also, as I mentioned, I was Type 1 diabetic and I inquired if he felt that it would be a hindrance. He reassured me that the several acting officers he knew with the disease were very effective and able to carry out their duties. So, he was very supportive of my attendance in his course, and we bonded somewhat with our "older" perspective of life.

As I write this exposé, I don't remember many of the students' names, nor where they ended up afterwards. One, Phil, became a good friend and he and I have stayed in contact ever since. He was the smallest member of our group, but had more passion and fire in his personality than all the rest. I often said later in my job as a Deputy Sheriff that the person I would want backing me up was Phil. He wasn't afraid to "mix it up" when necessary. His law enforcement career in itself warrants a book. He actually was elected to be Sheriff of Lewis County, Idaho.

I will diverge a bit from my story to relate one of his exposés shortly after he was elected Sheriff. He became somewhat known nationally via Paul Harvey's "The Rest of the Story". It still can be heard on the internet. Anyway, he was sitting on his front porch one day shortly after being elected Sheriff, and he observed some suspicious activity across the street. There was a pickup parked and it appeared to him that a drug deal was going down. So, he walked across to find out what was going on.

He asked the occupants "What are you doing here?"

They replied, "Go mind your own business!"

So as Paul Harvey in his own inimitable way said, "So, Sheriff Phil Steen did."

Phil went back home, put on his uniform and duty belt, returned, and arrested them for selling drugs.

This story highlights the bravado and confidence of a friend who I had the pleasure of knowing while serving in law enforcement. As the saying goes, "It's not the size of the dog in the fight, but the size of the fight in the dog."

I could say much about martial arts training, firearms training, officer safety training, but perhaps the most important part of our education was constitutional law. I didn't realize how ignorant I was about the foundation of our country regarding its basic tenets concerning the incredible wisdom employed in forming the system of government we have.

The United States of America is not a democracy! It is a republic. What does that mean? It means that by a majority vote, one side cannot abrogate the rights of the other side, ie. minority. By a simple one-vote majority, the majority cannot take away the rights of the lesser group. Whether there be an animus for one's skin color, religion, ethnicity, or sexual orientation, one's rights cannot be voted away by law. Only a change of the Constitution can accomplish that, and only through a very arduous process.

Benjamin Franklin, as well as the other Founders, knew what a democracy really was, to quote him:

"Democracy is two wolves and a lamb voting on what to have for lunch, while liberty is a well armed lamb contesting the vote!"

Throughout our history, we have had many abuses of people's rights. Voting rights of our black fellow citizens being the prime example. Citizens they are and were. It shows what ignorant non-vigilant citizens allow to happen. Our Founding Fathers knew through their prolific knowledge of history that a democracy was a bad form of government. They knew when they endorsed "We the people" to start off the Declaration of Independence, it meant that the people were preeminent in the best form of governance. They knew that "power corrupts," so to bind up those that governed, they put chains upon those that sought to govern. Our Republican form of government is the best that human beings have ever had. And as Benjamin Franklin is reported to have said to a woman who asked him what form of government they had created, he replied, "A republic, madam, if you can keep it."

Ben Franklin was absolutely correct. We, the people, must be the guardians of our own government and fate. That said it all. If we can keep it, meaning if we stay vigilant and educated enough to prevent those that govern from stealing from the governed their God given-rights.

Our education about constitutional law was a real eye-opener for me. Because it showed me how little I knew about my rights, and how abysmal our education system is in this country; that it shamefully fails to teach our children some of the most important information they should know. It is an absolute disgrace! I would say that ninety-five percent of the people in the U.S. are wretchedly ignorant.

I saw that every day in my time as a Deputy and it allowed us to legally abuse them of their constitutional rights. Anecdotal evidence of that will appear throughout this story. So, that being said, the most important part of my law enforcement training was knowing and comprehending the law.

One can probably survive well by not knowing the "Bill of Rights" from the sixth onward. However, be ignorant of the first five at one's own peril. I saw that clearly when I was an employed Law Enforcement Officer. I speak most emphatically about the fourth and fifth amendments.

The right of the people to be secure in their persons, houses, papers, and effects, against unreasonable searches and seizures, shall not be violated, and no Warrants shall issue, but upon probable cause, supported by Oath or affirmation, and particularly describing the place to be searched, and the persons or things to be seized.

Simply stated and quite clear in its meaning, the Fourth Amendment to the United States' Constitution is perhaps the second most important stated right of the people. In concept, it protects us against arbitrary intrusions into our lives by an aggressive and abusive government.

Throughout the history of our country, the limits have been pushed greatly by the myriad law enforcement agencies, albeit unsuccessfully in most instances when tried by the third branch of government, the judicial branch.

The Supreme Court and Appellate Courts in many instances have nullified many bad searches and seizures for various nefarious and incorrect actions by the police. The Fruits of the Poisonous Tree doctrine established by the Supreme Court in 1920 in the case Silverthorne Lumber Co. v. United States is one such ruling. It found that evidence gathered without a warrant or probable cause by the police is not admissible in court and usually will nullify the charge against the affected person or entity. With some exceptions, it is directly meant to prevent police misconduct.

While working as a Law Enforcement Officer I was imminently aware of the restrictions upon me and I was careful to not violate this right of the people. Later on I will relate a case of mine that involved the careful application of the Fourth to prevent a Poisonous Tree result.

So, in simple terms, what does it really mean?

First, what is probable cause? To have probable cause, an official of the government must have evidence that a crime has been committed or is about to be committed. It applies only to government entities, not private ones. For instance, a landlord might enter one's apartment in search of something pertaining to the renter, for whatever reason, and not be restricted by this amendment. He might be in jeopardy of other laws, such as burglary, if not permitted under the rental agreement.

But the point is the Fourth Amendment binds the actions of policing officials of any government agency. No one in any agency, local, state, nor federally sworn law officer or other, may usurp this right of the people.

So, even if the dog catcher wants to come onto your property to take your dog because of some complaint, he or she simply cannot without that warrant. He represents the power of that particular governmental agency and must abide by that amendment. So, educating oneself about this right is extremely important, and standing one's ground against the improper and illegal use of the law is paramount.

Normally, a Law Enforcement Officer will back down when one challenges them with "What is the probable cause of this stop?" be it in a car or walking down the sidewalk. A knowledgeable and vigilant citizenry will keep the government in check.

My hope in the writing of this book is that I can pass on interesting, humorous, and educational stories and information, and that the reader will better understand their rights in order to be "Secure (safe) in their persons, houses, papers, and effects."

The last part of the amendment specifies exactly how a search can be conducted. So an officer must swear or affirm an oath in front of a judge for what he wishes to search. If it is a gun, for instance, he cannot also search for drugs or anything else that is not specified in the warrant. However, if in the process of looking for that gun, he finds other illicit things, they are admissible, but only if they are found in the logical places to search. If it is a rifle that is specified, looking in a small drawer is not reasonable and such items would be thrown out by the court.

The Founding Fathers of our country were very smart and wise in carefully stating the words of each amendment. They had experienced the abuses of overbearing abusive governments and did all they could to protect the people. But as Mr. Franklin warned, it was the duty of the citizenry to be educated and vigilant in maintaining these rights and form of government. They knew it was good but required an involved people.

Abuses occur every day in law enforcement. Police take advantage of the ignorance of the people. It is like the wolves caring for the sheep. The herd can only be protected when it has guard dogs around it, ie. knowledge of their rights. Only with knowledge can the wolves be kept at bay. So I emphasize how important our rights are, as well as the will to use them.

Virtually all Law Enforcement Officers are decent people and take their jobs seriously. They will respect one's rights when confronted and stopped with the correct application of one's rights. Nobody wants to be sued in a court of law and a Law Enforcement Officer can be sued for violation of those rights. That lawsuit will start with the offending officer and include the agency for which he works and continue to the government body that controls that agency:

city, county, state, or federal. The Rodney King case in March of 1991 is a great example of police violating his rights and them being tried and found guilty. Although four officers were found not guilty by the state of California, the Federal Government tried them on a charge of violation of civil rights and two officers were found guilty and sentenced to prison. It was a real eye-opener for police officers to not violate the rights of those they swore to protect.

Probably the third most important right stated by Constitutional amendment is the Fifth Amendment:

No person shall be held to answer for a capital, or otherwise infamous crime, unless on a presentment or indictment of a Grand Jury, except in cases arising in the land or naval forces, or in the Militia, when in actual service in time of War or public danger; nor shall any person be subject for the same offense to be twice put in jeopardy of life or limb; nor shall be compelled in any criminal case to be a witness against himself, nor be deprived of life, liberty, or property, without due process of law; nor shall private property be taken for public use, without just compensation.

Perhaps a more complicated and hard to understand statement of rights, "pleading the fifth," as is well-known, protects us from incriminating ourselves. The famous case of Miranda vs. Arizona in 1966 by the U.S. Supreme Court forced all Law Enforcement Officers after an arrest or detention to state Fifth Amendment rights to the suspect or detainee. It came about because of ignorance. Ernesto

Miranda had not educated himself, like most citizens, on his constitutional rights; that he had the right to "keep his mouth shut!"

You have the right to remain silent. Anything you say can and will be used against you in a court of law. You have the right to talk to a lawyer for advice before we ask you any questions. You have the right to have a lawyer with you during questioning. If you cannot afford a lawyer, one will be appointed for you before any questioning if you wish. If you decide to answer questions now without a lawyer present, you have the right to stop answering at any time.

Again, ignorance on the part of the citizenry forced this outcome. Its meaning includes that whenever we are stopped by any Law Enforcement Officer, legally it is a stop under the Fourth Amendment, whether it be a traffic stop or when one is walking on a sidewalk, we have the right to not answer any question that could incriminate us.

Now, that doesn't mean if an officer stops us, we don't talk to them and answer non-investigative questions such as: "Are you having a nice day?", "Did you see someone leave their car here?" Being respectful and civil is always proper and conversing with any Law Enforcement Officer is good. But the moment they begin to question one about anything that could be a violation or criminal act, then it's time to clam up. Especially in traffic stops.

We all have been stopped for whatever infraction of driving. That traffic officer <u>must</u> have probable cause to stop a car as well. It is a seizure under the law. It can be for any reason such as speed, a car light that isn't functioning, or a myriad of other legal reasons according to the traffic laws of the state. An LEO is not permitted to stop someone simply because they feel like it. They **MUST** have probable cause!

Once one rolls down that window and sees the officer standing outside, your Fifth Amendment rights kick in. All one has to do is provide one's driver's license, vehicle registration, and proof of insurance as per all states' laws.

With questions like, "How fast were you driving?" "Have you been drinking?" or any other question that with one's answer will strengthen the officer's case, simply and respectfully say, "I prefer not to answer any of your questions." And if asked why, simply say that it is one's Fifth Amendment right not to.

I would surmise that in 99% of traffic stops, people incriminate themselves. They pay for their ignorance. The responsibility of proof of guilt is on the part of the state, or Law Enforcement Officer. They must prove that one violated the law. So shut up and make them do their job.

Also, keep things that might be a "problem" out of sight: such as drugs, guns, open liquor bottles, etc. If an officer sees something in one's car that is illegal or evidence of a crime it is called "plain view" evidence. He can charge one for this violation or even arrest that person or persons in the car. It constitutes probable cause.

Although one's vehicle is similar in status to a person's home, it is easier to do a search of the car because of visibility of what's inside and what can be done after an arrest. If a person is arrested after a traffic stop, then that vehicle cannot be left in place. It must be towed and therefore must be searched to secure and log the items inside. If anything illegal is found inside, then it adds to the list of charges. That has been reinforced by many Supreme Court and Appellate Court decisions.

Last, but not least of all of the enunciated rights, in fact the most important, is the Second Amendment.

A well regulated militia, being necessary to the security of a free state, the right of the people to keep and bear arms, shall not be infringed.

Much debated, much maligned, and much attacked, it is still intact. It is the one amendment that truly protects the whole document, meaning the Constitution. Many will debate its true purpose, but one only has to read the Federalist Papers to understand why the Founders included this amendment. It was to protect against evil tyrannical governmental authorities who seek to enslave the citizenry. The Founders had seen such chicanery throughout history and knew that if the government would be truly of the people, then the people needed power to keep it under control.

The famously recited truism, "When governments fear the people, there is liberty. When the people fear the government, there is tyranny," is without question rock-solid true. Those that wish to destroy this country and bring it under a "New World Order" or globalized government have one huge obstacle to overcome: eliminating the power of the citizenry to fight back.

We see multiple examples of despotic governments in modern times murdering millions of their citizens to exercise absolute control: Russia, Germany, China to name a few. First they took the guns, then the lives. It was wholesale butchery and slaughter to cow the people. But here in the United States of America, it is not easy to do that because of our Second Amendment.

Many unconstitutional laws have been nullified by the Supreme Court over the years, but governments still pass laws to "infringe" the right of the citizens to bear arms. What exactly does that word, "infringe," really mean? According to the Webster Dictionary: to encroach, defeat or frustrate, from the Medieval Latin, "infringere," to break or crush. From my perspective, it means *don't touch, hands off!* It takes vigilance and education to stop the illegal and immoral acts of legislators, both state and federal. Yet the mainstream propaganda machine still scandalizes stories of mass shootings by psychopaths and maniacs, all to inflame the emotions of the public. When the press refuses to report on the numerous times that lawful people have stopped crimes because of their right to have and carry a gun, it exacerbates the situation.

Guns don't kill people any more than cars kill people. People kill people. In England, where guns are totally prohibited, they kill each other with knives. Duh!!! It doesn't take a genius to see that people will kill each other forever with whatever means they have: knives, swords, baseball bats, hammers, chainsaws, even rocks (check your Bible on that one; it's called stoning).

The Second Amendment was not written for self-defense or hunting, but only for defense against a tyrannical government.

"The Constitution of most of our states (and of the United States) assert that all power is inherent in the people; that they may exercise it by themselves; that it is their right and duty to be at all times armed." – Thomas Jefferson, letter to John Cartwright, June 5, 1824

"A Free People ought not only be armed and disciplined, but they should have sufficient arms and ammunition to maintain a status of independence from any who might attempt to abuse them, which would include their own government." – George Washington

"To disarm the people...[i]s the most effectual way to enslave them." – George Mason, referencing advice given to the British Parliament by Pennsylvania governor Sir William Keith, The Debates in the Several State Conventions on the Adoption of the Federal Constitution, June 14, 1788

"Before a standing army can rule, the people must be disarmed, as they are in almost every country in Europe. The supreme power in America cannot enforce unjust laws by the sword; because the whole body of the people are armed, and constitute a force superior to any band of regular troops." – Noah Webster, An Examination of the Leading Principles of the Federal Constitution, October 10, 1787

"Necessity is the plea for every infringement of human freedom. It is the argument of tyrants; it is the creed of slaves." – William Pitt (the Younger), Speech in the House of Commons, November 18, 1783

The last quote by William Pitt best exemplifies what is happening today regarding mass shootings in our country. The politicians and press cry that it is necessary to take the guns from the citizenry. "We must stop this madness of killing poor innocent people. They can't be trusted." But it is their excuse for enslaving the people. The fact is criminals and madmen will always have guns. Only the citizenry will become sheep for the slaughter.

So, embrace what William Pitt said. "Don't give in to the soothsayers, charlatans and liars that want to enslave us. They are devils in disguise."

To add to these comments, I have never heard nor read about any public official, local, state, or federal and that includes elected persons, openly talk about the true reason for the Second Amendment. In Congress, the conservative members are constantly fighting against those that would diminish or eliminate this amendment, but they never talk about the importance of it against an overbearing government. It's always about self -defense or hunting. What a travesty!

It seems that individuals who have sworn an oath to defend the Constitution don't even understand it; or they willfully don't talk about it. If they did, we would never hear about it because the "presstitutes" of the mainstream media would

NEVER report it. Their controlling companies would fire them immediately. Truth is not what their profession is about. "We, the people" simply don't realize how blind and deceived we are. That is tragic!

I regard my education of the law and constitution as the most important part of my training. I too was ignorant! Not only did I learn how to apply the law, but how it should work in my personal life. I pulled away the veil of ignorance and saw clearly what a wonderful system of government we have been blessed with. It is absolutely unique in human history and probably the last and best one to test humankind if we can really rule ourselves well and peacefully.

All I can say after many words and stories is **KNOW YOUR RIGHTS!**

Chapter 4
Tactical Training

We had fun learning and practicing the use of firearms. Our main weapon, the sidearm, was the one most important for personal defense and stopping a criminal in his tracks. The school provided us with a Glock 17, 9 millimeter, but we had to buy our own duty belt, holster, two pairs of handcuffs, OC spray, expandable baton, PR 24 baton, and other accouterments of the profession. These are the most basic of needed tools for a Law Enforcement Officer.

In today's world, an officer needs these and many more items to do his job properly. The weight we carry can amount to 20 to 30 pounds or more, including our bulletproof vest. I never really had to work in hot weather areas, but when it was hot, I would arrive home totally soaked in my own sweat. For me, a true working police officer wore their vest under their uniform shirt, not like those in many Federal agencies where they don their bulletproof vest on the outside emblazoned with their agency name on the back: **FBI, BATF,** or **DEA**. They put on their vests when they go into action, whereas we were always "in action" and never knew when someone might try to harm or kill us.

These agencies liked to look down their noses at us local officers thinking we didn't know much, when in reality the opposite was true. We were ever vigilant 24/7, on duty and off. A Law Enforcement Officer is always a target, especially the local ones because people knew where we lived, and we were almost always out in our respective areas facing the citizenry. The "Federales" were protected two ways. They do not carry out dangerous arrests or investigations the entire time of their shift, nor do they live, generally speaking, in the areas they work. I know some would debate this characterization with me, so be it. I will relate an anecdotal story on this later.

If there was one thing we did constantly, it was to practice the proper use of our firearm. The purpose was to develop muscle memory and good eye hand coordination, ie. shoot well. Our instruction included the fact that most gunfights occur within ten feet, and only 18% of the bullets hit their mark. Why? Adrenaline that is pumped into our bodies during such a situation causes our muscles to do funny things, like "spaz out". So it was vital to develop a muscle memory of drawing and pointing our weapon properly without thinking. There is no time to think! One can only react to an offensive danger. As I related before, the time between action and reaction is at minimum .75 seconds, usually longer when one thinks. Our reaction to a deadly threat must be immediate and without thought, or we're dead or injured in such an encounter. That's why we practiced and often.

Proper muscle memory or reactionary action is critical in staying alive. The famous movie with Clint Eastwood, "Unforgiven", where his character, William Munny, went into the bar to kill Little Bill with his shotgun was a perfect example. The reaction of Bill's compatriots showed exactly what I am saying. After Little Bill was blasted to hell, they all started to shoot and were spraying bullets all over the place except at William. The adrenaline started flowing and they had no muscle memory nor training to deal with the situation.

When I first saw that scene, I thought, *Wow, the first true gunfight portrayed by Hollywood*. My point is this. We live it every day of our working career and if we want to go home safe after our shift to our family, we absolutely need to be well trained and prepared.

One of the questions asked of us before we started down the path of law enforcement was: "Are you prepared to take a life? If not, don't go down this path." Very few officers ever do kill someone, but the possibility is ever-present and we must be psychologically ready to do it. Whether we like it or not, that's the job and we must be ready to face and accept the consequences of our actions. Without resolute men and women prepared to either lay down their lives or take another, our civilization and way of life wouldn't last. Evil will always be with us and only righteous members of law enforcement or armies can thwart it.

Of course our training involved the use of many weapons and when to use them. A shotgun is utilized in deadly threat situations in close quarters. Its use is between a pistol and a long arm, or rifle. It can be used when there are multiple aggressors or when rifle accuracy and time can't be employed. A rifle takes some time to employ well. Find the target, sight in the target and fire. It's for distance. A shotgun will spray nine OO buckshot pellets a good 50 feet and hit the mark or two. It's for backup help or shear showdown power. There is nothing more fearsome and intimidating about facing a loaded shotgun than just a pistol. Crooks know that there is a chance of escape or survival with a pistol, especially a nine millimeter. For me, the nine millimeter caliber bullet is nearly worthless. It makes holes but really doesn't stop. The .40 caliber is the best because it has nearly the same stopping power as a .45 caliber with more bullets in the magazine. Anyway, one blast from a shotgun will stop any crazed PCP-loaded maniac. Shotguns are great in unruly crowd control; and loaded with rubber bullets they will put a real hurt on rioters.

More importantly, we learned proper use of force incrementation. Start low and move up the ladder as the situation escalates. We were trained in many types of counter-threat tools. At the low end is what is called "command presence". Just our uniform and how we present ourselves exudes authority. The Law Enforcement Officer is a servant of the people and their representative government. An officer is given authority by the government that hired him. We serve that government and the people it represents. We as officers are not the real power; the people are.

I personally lived by the adage that "Humility is the catalyst that makes power benevolent." So many young officers are arrogant and power-hungry. I saw it often where they thought the badge weighed 20 pounds and their chest stuck out to support it. Being that I was older and more worldly-wise, meaning I had had some of the shit kicked out of me along the way, I was more humbled and knew that "But by the grace of God go I." We must project authority to control situations and it starts with that uniform, badge and our bodily actions. The voice comes next. We start softly and with respect. If the situation escalates with defiance and anger, we must raise our level of command presence with more force. For example if we have a situation on the street where two are arguing and causing a scene, our approach is with a mild command such as "Please calm it down here." If after interaction with them the two continue, we must tell them to separate and stop arguing. If they ignore me, I might raise my voice and tell them "Stop, move away, **do it now!**" Use of voice commands are extremely important in controlling aggression and deescalating conflicts. Once things have calmed down, we can begin to sort them out and end the problem.

Unfortunately things don't always resolve themselves that way. Hot emotions drive anger to high levels, murder being the ultimate. As an event escalates in danger we too must escalate our force until it is controlled. The tools we use for less than lethal occurrences are: OC spray, baton, taser, and even rubber bullets. Rubber bullets hurt and OC burns. I know.

To be certified in the use of OC spray, we partnered up with a fellow trainee and sprayed each other with our own spray at point blank range. We had to keep our eyes wide open and receive a shot in our eyes, nose and mouth from a foot away. That was no fun! A half a second after it hit me, my eyes clamped shut and I began to spit and cough like never before. Snot came out of my nose like a long thick waterfall, and it was hard to breathe. During all of this, I had to force my left eye open with my left hand to see and draw my pistol to fend off the attacker. This was done by one and all to train us if our OC canister was removed from our belt and used against us. It was very unpleasant but very necessary. I remember it vividly to this day. It took fifteen minutes of hosing my face with water to return back to some normality. The red marks on my neck and chest stayed for a couple of days thereafter. I don't ever want to do it again, but it educated us on how effective and nonlethal a tool it is. I've only had to use it on dogs. They didn't like it either.

I won't elaborate too much on perhaps the next of nonlethal tools. There are two types of batons: the PR 24 and the expandable. I always carried on my duty belt the expandable baton because it was short and fit nicely on my left side. The PR 24 is the long black baton with a handle which is more commonly seen in movies. It has a long side and a short side. We have a ring on our duty belt to hang it, but we put it there only on special occasions. It stayed in my patrol car most of the time. The long side is for hitting someone's leg on the outside to affect the long nerve that runs along the thigh muscle or it can also be used on an arm. It shouldn't really be used to hit above the shoulders, for it can kill the victim. If one has to kill, there are better ways to do it. If the leg nerve is hit properly, it will buckle the leg and the victim will fall. Hitting on top of the arm will cause the hand to open and drop what is in it. The short end of the baton is for crowd control or unruly people that just don't get it. A swift poke in the ribs or stomach will usually back the person away. The expandable baton is strictly for hitting. I only had to pull it out once to get my point across. To deploy it, one must sling the open end of the baton down hard to fully extend it and raise it up above the shoulder to hit. In one instance, the person backed away quickly. He knew I meant business.

Again, these are tools that are used to control a bad situation. They are used when we face nonlethal events. What do I mean by that? It is when an officer is not likely to be severely injured or killed.

The final level is lethal use of force. By law and various court decisions, when is it righteous and legal to use one's firearm? Well, our training states that when a threat is within 21 feet and has something that can seriously injure or kill us, then that is the time to use deadly force. We use it to stop the threat, not to kill. If death results, then it sucks to be them. It is a situation when the threat is advancing and reaches that "21"-foot mark, or in reality, approximately that point, that we shoot. We are trained to double tap, or shoot twice, and evaluate. If the threat continues, double tap again. We do that until the threat stops. 21 feet is the distance that was legally and professionally established to give the officer time to react to the threat. It was found that an aggressor can advance that distance quickly enough and not give an officer a lot of time to react. Again, the action versus reaction time comes into play. The aggressor can have a knife, baseball bat, hammer, or anything that can seriously injure or kill us. Within that distance, we don't warn or say "freeze" or any other bullshit that Hollywood likes to use; we just shoot. I want to go home alive and well.

Now, if a gun is used outside that distance and if it is pointed at me, I shoot and ask questions later. I'm sure that before such a situation is faced, there has been an effort to prevent the suspect from going there. But once they do lethal force must be used. It is either them or me.

Again, hesitation is a killer. We are trained to think about various scenarios and what to do when confronted with such. Pre-thinking various situations helps eliminate having to think at a moment when there isn't time. We must react, not ponder on what to do. So running various scenarios through our thoughts helps create a cognitive dissonance that kicks in with the adrenaline. It helps us draw that weapon quickly and shoot straight. Training is the key to keeping one safe whether in law enforcement or the military. The Law Enforcement Officer has a family to return home to.

I might add a sad thought process that I have noticed in recent police encounters. It seems that too many LEOs are going straight to their guns in situations that don't require deadly force. Apparently lack of proper training in force escalation is becoming common and the officer goes straight to their gun instead of OC, taser, or other less than lethal weapon. I'm sure massive lawsuits have been the result.

Look up, look down, look all around. I learned this

important lesson by failing in a building search exercise. Doing building searches is an important part of the job. My first chapter exemplified that well. We worked in pairs with one in front and one in back. When entering any doorway, the front officer focused forward, scanning left to right and back. With our gun pointed in the direction of our eyes and moving with them, the front man handles threats forward. The second officer behind does the same, only watching our backs. In other words, we are observing our entire perimeter.

This day, we entered a stairwell in an office building. I cautiously opened the door and proceeded inward with my compatriot right behind. I looked up the stairway and underneath and as we both fully entered, we heard "Bang, bang, you're dead." The training officer had straddled himself just above the doorway on a small ledge and shot us with his simulated plastic gun. Boy, were we surprised and embarrassed. I don't think any of our group passed the test that day. But did it ever cement in my mind to look up. The whole exercise was for us to be ever-vigilant and aware of our surroundings; to be situationally aware.

I am going to repeat that: **BE SITUATIONALLY AWARE!**

The people of the modern world today are oblivious to their surroundings. There are too many laughable examples on YouTube of people walking along a sidewalk staring at their telephones, without a clue of what is going on around them, banging into poles or worse, getting hit by a car when they cross the street. This is lamentable! As well, people get robbed or killed because they are taken by surprise by cunning criminals waiting for such a JAFI to pass by. Like a lion, they jump on these hapless fools and do their nefarious deeds.

Oh, by the way, one might want to know what is a JAFI: Just another f...king idiot! I coined this acronym years ago while observing and dealing with stupid, vapid behavior.

Anyway, back to the point. Especially now in an ever-increasingly dangerous world, it is vitally important to be aware of what is going on around us. If after reading this tome, one learns one lesson; being situationally aware is tops. It can be a life-saver. To this day, I am always looking around to see what is there, noting anomalies, things that don't belong or are simply out of place. When traveling in cities or other unfamiliar places, I always and frequently look behind me. It is second nature and vital to remaining safe on the job, or civilian life as well. It may not be as much a matter of personal safety in most situations as personal loss of property. Pickpockets, and con men use distraction techniques to rob people.

Again, being aware of one's surroundings is prudent when staying safe and sound. It is so common now to see people so oblivious to what is happening around them when "mated" to their cell phone. They are easy pickings and prone to injury or death with the distraction of a cell phone. It is only one example of not being situationally aware. We as humans tend to look frontward and down, occasionally to the side and rarely up.

Our training was designed to overcome that trait. Looking

up, down and all around was a motto that kept me safe and aware of what was happening in my vicinity since a person in uniform becomes the focus of attention of the people nearby.

Officer safety was pounded into us. Go home alive and well at the end of your shift. It is what truly matters when the day is done. Your loved ones await you. So it became second nature to have eyes in the back of our heads. Look up, look down, look all around, repeatedly! More and more, we are hearing about police officers being ambushed, shot, attacked with machetes and killed. We learned from examples of such events to be aware of the cunningness of evil and how to avoid it.

For example, one officer was killed during a traffic stop when after approaching the vehicle, an assailant popped out of the trunk and shot the officer. What a tragic and unforeseen occurrence. But that officer's inattention to an abnormality with the slightly-opened trunk is what cost him his life and probably saved the lives of many other officers. That mistake was included in our training and I always checked the trunk of cars I stopped. It was a perfect example of "expect the unexpected". It heightened my observance of all that was unusual or out of place in all stops of vehicles and people. Although most citizens view police officers as their friend, many do not. Some have a burning hatred for authority figures, and at the top of the list are LEOs . We were taught that as soon as we became one, we became a target, both on and off duty. So officer safety was pounded into us. I know, I sound like a broken record, but repetition is good.

Aside from situational awareness, second to this was to protect the weaponry you carry. In other words, don't let anyone take your "goodies." The most dangerous weapon an officer carries is his sidearm, or pistol for those that don't know what that is. Always, always protect that gun! A lax posture will get an officer killed. So, when talking to someone, an officer must position his body so the gun side is away from the person involved. It makes it harder for someone to grab the gun and shoot. One's hands also must be unoccupied to be able to respond to a threat quickly. A Deputy's gun is or always should be chambered with a round as to be fired quickly. So, anyone grabbing it will be able to shoot and empty the magazine full of bullets on the officer. Oh, boy, that would be a bad day even with a bulletproof vest. Kidding aside, it has happened too many times with careless, inattentive officers that have been shot with their own weapons. If others involve themselves in a Deputy's conversation with a person, the Deputy must move to keep both and all others in front and protect that pistol. Again, situational awareness comes into play. Stay safe! I could relate many other aspects of good officer safety training but in general it is all about the awareness of being a target.

Becoming a good Deputy meant learning the law, both state and federal, and being able to apply it quickly and correctly regarding the crime involved. Lawyers have the luxury of time to assign a criminal code to the actual crime, but a Deputy only has minutes to correctly assess the event and detain or arrest based on that knowledge of codified law. Laws are always changing and new ones are being added. I became a Deputy Sheriff and was responsible to know not only the extensive set of criminal laws but also traffic laws.

We as Deputies had to know everything about all facets of law enforcement: traffic, investigations, domestic violence, drugs, and much more. We did it all, whereas many larger departments have separated those functions. Specialization has become the norm if the money is available. So it was that our duty incorporated all areas of law enforcement.

Yes, there were times when we needed help from more knowledgeable sources. A good example was when stopping a large semi truck and trailer for some infraction I would call on an officer from the ISP, Idaho State Patrol, for assistance. Their responsibilities were more focused on traffic control and Federal Department of Transportation regulations. I would handle the infractions committed under state law and turn over to the ISP officer infractions committed under Federal law such as travel logs, weights, and proper loading. They are specialized and trained in those areas. Also major accident reconstruction was an area we left to them. When major investigations into a crime were needed, we turned it over to a detective, either in our agency or to the state which had a far more extensive facility to handle such crimes.

The point is we still had to know and be well-versed in all areas of law enforcement and know when to recruit additional help. It was a fun job from the standpoint that each day presented new challenges instead of a more routine specialization.

Our training ended in the classroom and transitioned to intern with various local law enforcement departments. I worked at the Jerome County Jail, the Kimberly City Police Department, and finally the Twin Falls County Sheriff's Department. For about a week, each stint we were able to apply our knowledge in real-life working situations, like what a doctor would do after years of medical schooling. There is nothing like hands-on work to cement what one has learned in the classroom. We were all rated by the various agencies we worked under and in the end "Grandpa" won the top prize.

The award for being the top student in the College of Southern Idaho's Law Enforcement Program was a new protective bulletproof vest; it was not a cheap award. I can truly say that it was the best spent year in higher education in my life; it has served me well since.

Chapter 5
Going to Work

After a long year of training at the College of Southern Idaho in Twin Falls, and interning with various departments in the area, I was ready to "spread my wings." There were several avenues of law enforcement to pursue: working in a jail, which many officers had to do before getting onto the patrol force, city law enforcement, state enforcement, which required additional training, or county. For me, being a Deputy under an elected Sheriff was my preference. I knew it involved working the whole county and doing everything. That included all cities in the county, all rural parts, and all federal lands. A Sheriff and his Deputies are not restricted on where they go, except in some states where there are top secret installations which federal authorities handle.

A Sheriff is the supreme law enforcement authority in his county, and no other agency, local, state, nor federal can usurp that authority. The Sheriff is an elected office and is sovereign in his county. Such so that in the state of Idaho, and in most other states, only a specified person can arrest the Sheriff; in Idaho the County Coroner, and only upon probable cause and warrant issued by a court.

What seems to be an archaic law was based on old west law. The Sheriff was king in his county. However, once he left the county, he was like everyone else, fair game. Now, one might ask "why is that?" Well, simply put, it was to protect the rights of the citizens who elected him. They had the confidence to put the person in that position and didn't want him to be threatened or influenced by outside forces, sometimes corrupt ones. It is a good law to keep outside agencies from violating the rights of the citizens within the county. Several recent Federal Court decisions have reinforced the authority of the Sheriff by attempts from the federal agencies to override a Sheriff's authority.

A perfect example of that was the case that Sheriff Dave Mattis brought against the BATF and IRS: Case #96-CV099-J, U.S. District Court, District of Wyoming, where he fought against those agencies for usurping his authority. His job was to protect his citizen's rights against abuses by these federal agencies and he won. I include below an article by the Knoxville Journal about the case. It says it better than I and is important to be read by all.

Knoxville Journal, pA1 and A6
August 7–13, 1997

SHERIFF BOOTS FEDS FROM HIS COUNTY
by Phil Hamby

Sheriff Dave Mattis of Big Horn County, Wyoming, said this week that as a result of Case #96-CV099-J, U.S. District

Court, District of Wyoming, he now has a written policy that forbids federal officials from entering his county and exercising authority over county residents unless he is notified first of their intentions.

After explaining their mission, Mattis said he grants them permission to proceed if he is convinced they are operating within the legal parameters and authority limitations set forth in the U.S. Constitution.

The sheriff grants permission on a case-by-case basis only. When asked what, if any, repercussions he had gotten from the Feds, he quickly and confidently replied, "None whatsoever." He explained by saying, "They know they do not have jurisdiction in my county unless I grant it to them."

Mattis clarified his position by saying the Federal Court had ruled the state of Wyoming is a sovereign state and the state constitution plainly states that a county sheriff is the top law enforcement official in the county.

Additionally, Sheriff Mattis contends that the U.S. Constitution, Article 1, Section 8, clearly defines the geographic territories where the Federal government has jurisdiction. Amendment X, he said, states that "the powers not delegated to the United States by the Constitution, nor prohibited by it to the States, are reserved to the States respectively, or to the people."

Therefore, Mattis thoroughly believes the Feds have very limited powers in any state unless the local high-sheriff allows them to exercise power beyond that which the Constitution provides.

"Put another way," Mattis said, " if the sheriff doesn't want the Feds in his county, he has the constitutional power and right to keep them out or ask them to leave."

Accompanied with other legal interpretations Mattis stands on the definition of the word "sovereign," which is defined by Webster's as "paramount, supreme. Having supreme rank or power, Independent: a sovereign state."

Mattis said he grew weary of the Feds coming into his county and running rough-shod over county residents: i.e., illegally searching and seizing property, confiscating bank accounts, restricting the free use of private lands and other abuses, without a valid warrant and without first following due process of law as guaranteed by the Constitution to every citizen.

As long as Mattis remains sheriff he says he will continue to see to it that the citizens of his county get their day in court.

Mattis went on to say that, to his knowledge, even the IRS has not attempted to seize any citizen's real property, bank account or any other private-owned possessions since he ran the Feds out of his county.

Sheriff Mattis emphasized that he is not a radical man. He said he is only dedicated to protecting the constitutional rights of the citizens of his county. He added that ordinary citizens are not the only ones bound by and expected to obey laws. Elected Officials and government employees at all levels of government are also bound by and should be expected to obey certain laws.

As long as Sheriff Mattis is the high-sheriff of Big Horn County, he seems determined to make sure private citizens and government officials alike act within the law and their designated powers.

Sheriff Mattis came across as a soft-spoken, polite man whose only interest is protecting the citizens he was elected to serve. That being the case, he might be the sheriff for as long as he wants to be.

Sheriff Mattis is hopeful that other sheriffs will assume the same stance. c. 1997 The Knoxville Journal

The purpose of including this article as written is to show how important it is for us all to know our rights. We are constantly being bombarded by efforts of various state and federal governmental agencies to restrict our rights. Throughout history we have seen, as well as our Founding Fathers, that governments cannot be trusted. No matter how clear a law is, especially in the Bill of Rights, evil, tyrannical, and corrupt elected and unelected officials try to infringe on those rights.

No better example of this is the current attempt by many state legislatures to infringe on the right of the people to bear arms. Even after multiple decisions by the Supreme Court of the United States and other Appellate Courts against such infringements, states such as New York and California continue to thumb their nose at the ultimate decider of our laws, the Supreme Court. It is for that reason that the Founding Fathers included in the Bill of Rights the Second Amendment. Principally it was not meant to be a self-defense nor hunting right but rather one to protect us from a corrupt and tyrannical government. As stated previously in this writing, the originators of the Constitution knew that only a well-armed citizenry would prevent such overreach by its government.

With all that in mind, I set out to be on the team of a Sheriff in one of the 44 counties in Idaho. I love the outdoors and beauty that is Idaho and began applying in various departments.

I'm going to interject a bit of my personal ideology. I am a staunch believer in keeping the Sabbath day holy (Saturday for me) as God commanded us in the fourth Commandment. I won't elaborate more but only want to say it was a big wall to get around when hiring on as a LEO in any governmental agency. In the interview process of virtually every agency I applied to, the question was always asked if I was able to work every day of the week. Of course, I answered that question with a negative because of the Sabbath day restrictions. I was turned down by many, even though I was the top of my class and had more maturity than the younger applicants.

Then I was interviewed by a newly-elected Sheriff for Mountain County in the west central part of Idaho. I was interviewed by Tom, the Under Sheriff, and others and the interview went well. Strangely, they never asked the question, and as a result I was hired. Upon getting set up with the department, I "came clean". Tom was not really happy about it, but he knew he was stuck.

Title VII of the Civil Rights Act was my protection against discrimination for religious beliefs. Only if by hiring me it would cause undue hardship for the department would the department have cause to release me. Tom asked me really only one pertinent question regarding the situation. What if there was a legitimate emergency on the Sabbath day and I was needed? I replied "I will be the first officer out there helping." Why? Wouldn't that be a break of my faith? I explained that an emergency is an entirely different situation than a normal scheduled work day. It is good to do good on the Sabbath day. The proverbial example of helping the cow out of the ditch on the Sabbath day is a perfect reflection of the concept. Even though it is work, it is always good to help others in serious need of help. It is a good thing.

And as Jesus explained to his disciples, "The Sabbath was made for man, not man for the Sabbath." That reply to Tom opened the door for me and started a career in what was the favorite endeavor of my life. Tom and his wife, Connie, who worked at the department, became good friends. We were the older folks of the department and we had much in common. More on that later.

So began my law enforcement career involving a department I loved and a beautiful place to work. As I continue with this story, the reader will understand.

Chapter 6
Coming up to Speed

As in all jobs, one has to "learn the ropes". What does that phrase mean? It means learning how a job is done well, learning about all facets of a particular job. It came from old nautical instruction for newcomers on a ship to learn basic information about the various ropes used on it. I often wonder about many of the phrases we use in modern language, so even I had to look up the origin and meaning of this phrase. It is a good phrase that I believe most people understand in whatever job they are employed and "learning the ropes" in any job is critical to doing something well.

So it was with me as well, learning how things operated and were done correctly with this Sheriff's Department. We had three Sergeants on the force that instructed me in how things were done according to what the new Sheriff wanted. Naturally, things didn't change much from what previous Sheriffs did, but there are always new things to learn when a new one takes over. So, to start with, I was issued a set of uniforms, badge, and identity.

I became Deputy 2114 (twenty-one fourteen). We used our identifier number when communicating with our Dispatch Department and others in public. Of course, my name badge was Deputy Anderson, but while communicating with Dispatch, it was always by number. Our county seat was Buffalo, Idaho where the offices and jail were located. When calling by radio, either in my patrol car or by handheld, I would say simply "Buffalo, 2114". This would tell Dispatch that they were being called by me; short and simple.

They would reply "2114," which meant I was heard and to continue with my inquiry. Keeping conversations short and simple was important because not only were Deputies calling in, but also other agencies. This was an important part of learning how things worked.

I rode with my various Sergeants for weeks before they cut me loose to work alone. Joe, who was the senior Sergeant, Matt, and Bill were all great instructors.The whole process was great fun, riding with different guys who had their own style. I might add a commentary about Joe. Initially he was a real "hard ass" because he was part of the hiring process and didn't like that I wasn't straightforward in my religious needs. He intended to work me over, make it tough. But in the end, I won him over. We became good comrades. He was closer to my age and respected my maturity and viewpoints. Most of the time they were working with younger guys (at that time there were no female patrol officers), who were harder to tame and instruct. As I said before, life experience has a way of kicking the shit out of us and humbling us. The younger ones weren't there, yet.

Simply learning to drive a patrol car is an interesting experience. As I mentioned previously, mine was a Ford Explorer with a substandard engine for such a vehicle, and a caged compartment in the back with a hard plastic seat formed to fit the shape of the body. Comfortable seats weren't part of the package. Vomiting, pissing, and crapping "customers" were part of the job and such a seat made it easier to clean up the mess.

The vehicle had ample storage room in the back for emergency supplies and other accouterments of the job. I liked this vehicle instead of pickups that were purchased later with more usable room under-roof. In addition was of course our radio, and in later units came the computer with access to Dispatch to check drivers' licenses and vehicle license plates directly without involving a Dispatcher. The computers really helped alleviate the workload of the Dispatchers. In between the front seats were two gun racks to hold a shotgun with 00 buck shot rounds and an AR 15 rifle with .223 bullets. Of course the patrol vehicle had the appropriate signage on the doors and lights and siren above.

Tom, the Under Sheriff, did a lot of the improvements on our vehicles. He was the department's handyman.

"Speed," the word we were trained to control. The greatest hazard and liability faced by any county is that of an accident incurred by one of its Law Enforcement Officers. An out-of-control, speeding patrol vehicle driven by an inexperienced Deputy which causes an accident resulting in injury or death can cost the county millions of dollars.

It can be devastating to all those concerned. This was the prime reason for training by the Sergeants in observing our abilities and caution.

During P.O.S.T. (Police Officer Standards & Training) education, we went through various skid car training and obstacle courses. We were trained to look far ahead and to observe what was happening; to anticipate. Complacency and inattention could be killers. So it was vital to be ever-aware; again, situational awareness. So, when running code 2, lights only, or code 3, lights and siren, we were pushing the limit of speed and care. Although an emergency vehicle running under these codes had the right of way regarding all traffic, an officer still had to be careful. By law, all vehicles had to stop and pull to the side of the road to allow any emergency vehicle to pass. Unfortunately that was not always the case. Many vehicles would fail to pull over, especially when we were following. The drivers either couldn't hear us or see us. Most drivers don't look in their rearview mirror as often as they should. Some are simply too obstinate and stupid to give the right of way. Whichever, it is a citable misdemeanor offense and can result in a huge fine or jail time. Regardless, when running code, we don't have time or interest in such foolishness. However, later I will relate a serious story about one such driver.

So, when driving in this manner we had to be very cautious and alert, especially at intersections. Although running a patrol unit with lights and siren gives the officer right of way in all situations, when entering an intersection with stop lights, the driver must slow down to alert the public and advance only when safe. Too many times accidents occur when the emergency vehicle enters an intersection against a red light without slowing sufficiently to give cars time to stop when they think it's a green light for them. We had to be very mindful of this when running code 3.

From the start, I was issued my own patrol vehicle which I drove from my home. The training Sergeants always rode with me and monitored my handling of the vehicle. It was their job to verify to the Sheriff that I was a safe and responsible driver. They would also assist me on traffic stops by backing me up on the opposite side of the detained vehicle. It was their job to get a new recruit up to speed.

As explained before, radio communication was meant to be as concise as possible utilizing 10 code; ie. 10-4 meant "message received and acknowledged."

I would often request a 10-27 on a particular driver's license. My conversation with Dispatch would go something like: "Buffalo 2114" and they would reply only "2114," which acknowledged my call. I would continue "My 10-20 is mile marker 18, Hwy 55, 10-28 on Idaho plate V 12345, red Dodge pickup." Dispatch would reply "copy" and get back to me with particular information on that vehicle and owner. I succinctly told them that I had stopped a red Dodge pickup at that location, and wanted information on that vehicle before I approached it.

More often than not, nothing negative would come back. But sometimes the vehicle would have expired plates or worse, be stolen. If the latter was the case, I would not approach the vehicle until I had requested backup and the backup was on scene. I and my fellow officer would then approach the vehicle under a felony stop situation; which meant guns drawn and ordering the driver out of the vehicle. The whole felony stop scenario was dangerous and it involved a whole special set of procedures. It was one of those times when a Deputy's adrenaline amped up. But thank God very few stops were like that.

After receiving from Dispatch the necessary information about the vehicle, I would exit my patrol unit and walk to the driver's side window but not directly across from the driver, but slightly behind to observe inside the vehicle, after checking the trunk to see if it was open. First and foremost, if no one else was inside I looked for the hands of the driver to see where they were. I especially wanted to clearly see his right hand. If I couldn't, I would request the driver to put both hands on the steering wheel. The right hand was the hand that could kill me, either with a pistol or knife if I was too close. Assuring myself that I was not in danger, I would proceed with my conversation about the stop. During a traffic stop, I had detained the citizen under Fourth Amendment guidelines. I would explain to the driver my reason for the stop, the probable cause likely a violation of traffic codes. I would ask for their driver's license, registration, and proof of insurance; all the time that the driver was acquiring those documents, I was observing things and smells from inside the car. Then the process of how far I could go began.

Before I continue with that, I want to repeat to the reader that under Fourth Amendment law, they are being detained. At that point, their Fifth Amendment rights kick in. Other than kind and noncommittal conversation, they should keep their mouths shut. Don't admit to anything! If I ask if they know how fast they were going, don't answer. Simply say, "I prefer not to answer any questions," because if the driver says they were driving just one mile over the limit, they have admitted they violated the law. Although that is a fairly innocuous admission, admitting to drinking just one beer, if asked how much they have had to drink, can open a "whole can of worms".

All traffic officers will attempt to get one to admit to things they shouldn't. "Have you been drinking? Do you have any illegal substances in the vehicle? How fast were you driving?" etc. By asking those and similar questions, the officer is trying to get the detainee to admit to a violation or crime. It simply makes the officer's job easier. **Don't do that!!** One has the right to remain silent. The concept of the Miranda law isn't only for criminal arrests. It is for traffic violations as well. So, give the officer your documents and don't answer possible incriminating questions. The only citizens that seem to know that are lawyers. I have a good anecdotal story about that later, when I almost pushed too far and got into trouble.

While working with Sergeant Matt one day, I made a stop outside of a small town on the main highway that transited through the county. As we were approaching the town, a car was leaving at a rate of speed that I visually estimated at about 15 miles per hour over the posted speed limit. I used my front facing radar to check the car's speed and sure enough my estimate was correct. So I turned on my overhead lights, did a quick turn, and stopped the car. I went through the appropriate communication with Dispatch and heard nothing that would be a problem with it. I and Matt exited the patrol car and approached the driver's side, with him approaching the passenger side. The driver had his license out and I asked for his other papers. I then told him that he was 15 mph over the limit; that was the reason for the stop.

He pleaded "Man, I know I was speeding but I was just accelerating out of town. It's my birthday today, can't you give me a break?"

I told him to stay with the car and that I would return shortly. I saw that he was immediately dejected and hung his head. I sat back in the patrol car with Matt and confirmed that indeed it was his birthday. I began writing the citation. I stopped and looked at Matt and asked him "What do you think?" He simply smiled and shrugged his shoulders.

I sat for a moment, thinking, and then scribbled out what I had written on the citation. My heart wasn't into giving this guy a ticket. It was his birthday. So we both returned to the car and I gave the man his documents and said,

"Look, I know it's your birthday today and I'm giving you a present. I'm not going to cite you for the infraction even though normally I would. So, happy birthday. But please do me a favor by keeping your speed down and within reason. Don't go down the road and do the same thing and make me look like a fool."

After his profuse thank you, we returned to the patrol unit. I sat down and looked at Matt, expecting his opinion.

He simply said "That was cool." His comment meant the world to me. This story was easy to recall because of Matt's approval. Throughout my career I made hundreds of stops and I remember few, but this was at the top.

What's my point for this story? Number one, we as Deputies are servants to the people. Our job is to help when able, and to take corrective action with humility. It is not our job to punish; that is the job of the courts. I always fall back on my favorite adage, "Humility is the catalyst that makes power benevolent."

So, what would I have accomplished if I had given the man a ticket? I would have ruined his day and made an enemy. That's not my job. Our job as Deputies was to gain compliance with the law and a favorable view of the Mountain County Sheriff's Department. I was in the "sales" business. As mentioned before, my ability to sell my "product" was just as important as if I was selling chemicals to a customer. It is very important to view the job from that perspective in order to gain compliance; something younger Deputies didn't know about. We wanted the public to "love us", or maybe that's a little extreme. However, it's essential that the citizens of the county trust us and aren't afraid to call for help, or to simply say hello when we encounter them on the street. That's our job.

In this situation, I felt I made a positive attitude towards the birthday boy and he would be more conscious in obeying traffic laws. In all my encounters I never told someone to go the speed limit. That's ridiculous. Nobody does that all the time, and moreover we don't expect drivers to perfectly stick to the limit. Only to be reasonable with their driving and speed.

Here's a tip for readers who drive. Generally, a traffic officer is going to give a grace of five miles over the limit. But beware of going more than that. My limit was ten over the limit before I would stop a vehicle. Normally I wouldn't issue a citation at that speed, but it gave me the opportunity to check for other infractions or crimes. Top of the list were expired tabs for license plates, suspended driver's license, and an outstanding warrant.

I am going to inject some additional information about the equipment we carried in the patrol car, which I left out previously. I had a radar that had front and back antennas. We could measure the speed of traffic both coming and going. So if a vehicle was close to the limit of excessive speed heading toward me, I might check after the vehicle passed to see if it began to accelerate. Normally drivers tend to slow down or brake when a patrol unit approaches, and then after passing my vehicle, they might speed up again. With my rear-facing antenna I could measure their speed when leaving behind me. Then I would turn and pursue them if they made that mistake.

Like Gomer Pyle, I would say "Surprise, surprise." When making a stop using our radar we were required by the Court to have a good visual estimate of the speed before we triggered the radar. It was a requirement that made us establish a probable cause for further action; the radar simply justified what we observed. It took practice and the Sergeants were always emphasizing and testing us on our speed judgment. For those who might doubt the accuracy of the radar unit, we always checked both antennas on every shift with a tuning fork. The sound frequency represented the return frequency of an approaching vehicle at a specific speed. Therefore the driver couldn't claim that the radar unit wasn't showing the correct speed. Generally it was within two percentage points accurate.

It wasn't long before I was up to standards on what was expected of a Patrol Deputy. After two months I was cut loose to go on my own. It was my show from then on.

Chapter 7
Doing the job

We worked four ten-hour shifts, which I loved. My schedule was usually Sunday through Thursday, which gave me three free days. There were two shifts that ran during the day, from 7:00 am to 5:00 pm, and 5:00 pm to 3:00 am.

I preferred the night shift. Usually there was more going on and my forte was finding drunk drivers during the "witching hours" from 10:00 pm to 2:00 am. That is when most problems occurred, particularly drunk drivers. I became adept at hunting them.

Now, I will be the first to say that during my youth, I admit that I drove several times when I should not have. My own experiences taught me valuable lessons about driving under the influence, (DUI). It is a common situation where after hours of drinking in a bar, one thinks one is able to drive home. I could relate several of my own driving while drunk experiences, but I'd rather not. Suffice it to say, I have been there and done that. I knew that it was dangerous and must be controlled to maintain safety on the highways and streets.

DUI in the state of Idaho included alcohol, drugs, and even medication. Anything that could impair one's ability to drive safely was "verboten" (forbidden). Now, in other states they called it DWI or driving while intoxicated, meaning alcoholic beverages. But I'm sure those laws are more encompassing. The limits of intoxication or inebriation in most states, if not all, are guided by Federal law. The states decide their own laws, however, but because they receive a lot of money from the Federal Government for transportation expenses, such as building and maintenance of highways, they are pressured to abide by Federal standards.

So, most states regard a blood alcohol content of .08 mg per dl (miligrams per deciliter) as the point where a driver is considered DUI. At that point, any law enforcement officer may and should arrest a driver found driving a vehicle or even behind the wheel, in control of the vehicle but stopped. For underaged drivers and commercial drivers, the limits are even stricter.

So, what does .08 B.A.C. even mean? Well, for example, a male weighing approximately 170 lbs. that has consumed four drinks in an hour would be at the limit. It all depends on the weight of a person and the strength of the beverage. Generally a cup of wine, a bottle of beer, and a shot of whiskey equal about the same punch. Four of either in an hour will put a driver at the limit. Normally, the human body will burn off a drink in an hour, but if one continues to consume at the rate explained, then the B.A.C.

goes up and it just gets worse. The drinking catches up on one and eventually by the time it's over, people don't have the ability to discern their inebriation. Then they go out and drive. It is a common occurrence and our job was to try and stay on top of it before people were killed.

A very sad story of such an event happened to a good friend of mine with the Idaho State Patrol. ISP officers covered all of the highways in the state of Idaho. Their job was mostly traffic control. I got to know Tim with the ISP through various backup needs, either for him or myself. The law enforcement community is a pretty tight group of people that help each other. Whether it be city, county, state or federal officers, we knew each other and worked together on many occasions.

So, it was that one night while I was working that I got word that a very bad accident had occurred in the neighboring county. A drunk driver failed to stop at the intersection to a main highway and slammed into a vehicle, actually T-boned the vehicle, and killed four people. Tim was the first officer on scene and of those dead, there were three children. The horror he saw was unimaginable. He had to work through that tragedy and it took a long time for him to recover. The disastrous result of drunk driving is a daily occurrence throughout the nation. It made me resolute in doing all that I could to ameliorate the numbers of such events.

I really enjoyed the day shifts as well because I would start out by stopping at the Sheriff's office and talking to the front office personnel, Patti, the main front desk officer, Connie, and her husband, Tom, the Under Sheriff. Having a cup of coffee and discussing the day's events with them was a joy. It started the day off well. Connie and I were always playing word games and one day I casually used a word she didn't know. I told her I had an "epiphany" about something about which I don't recall and she exclaimed "What is that word?" I beamed with delight explaining to this crossword puzzle fanatic what it meant. She was surprised and just laughed and said "You're a pretty smart guy."

I had great fun stealing from their bag of pretzels she always had by the desk. I surprised them one day by bringing in a new bag from Costco.

Patti, though, was really the heart of that office and knew everything about everything. She ran a tight ship, which helped the Deputies a lot when we needed something. Years after I left the department, she was voted in as Sheriff and still is as of this writing. I would have loved to have worked for her. I'm sure she is a great Sheriff because she was a great manager, which is what a Sheriff really is supposed to be. One who manages all the various departments under them: jail operations, patrol operations, emergency responders (ambulance and search and rescue), finances, interaction with the county commissioners and attorney, and much more. A good Sheriff is a good manager.

The Sheriff for whom I worked was a bad Sheriff. Tony came from Tennessee and was hired by the previous Sheriff to be a detective. How he ended up in Idaho I do not know; he was kind of a misfit in that part of the country. Anyway, he was elected to be the Sheriff after the previous one ran into trouble with a DUI in his own county. As I remarked earlier about arresting a Sheriff in his own county, the situation was handled with "kid gloves" by an ISP officer. Word got out quickly and that ended his career. The citizens of Mountain County didn't like their Sheriff driving drunk and sent him packing shortly thereafter in the next election.

Tom, the Under Sheriff, was the person that really got Tony elected through a well-orchestrated campaign. As a result, Tony made Tom the Under Sheriff. It should have been the other way around. Although Tom had no P.O.S.T. training, he was a quick study and was well-liked in the department. He was unpretentious and humorous but also attentive to the needs of the Patrol Officers. He was the one that mostly dealt with the County Commissioners trying to squeeze money from them to help the department.

Everyone knew that Tony had a sword of Damocles hanging over his head regarding a fish and game violation. The Department of Natural Resources was after him. Eventually, not knowing for sure, the pressure convinced him to resign his office under the pretext of a better job. That involved going to Kosovo as a UN police officer. It was very unusual and suspicious that a sitting Sheriff only three years into his term would do that. He evidently saw the handwriting on the wall or was given an ultimatum. He bowed out gracefully.

Of course, the resignation caused a big stir in the department and the Commissioners were tasked with choosing a new Sheriff. Tom was the likely logical choice, but for unknown reasons, the Commissioners chose someone else, a Detective within the department. For me, it was a huge slight to Tom for all the work he had done and a stupid decision on the part of the Commissioners. What behind the scenes finagling went on is anyone's guess, but we all knew it was a kick in the pants to Tom and Connie. They left the department shortly after. Losing Tony was a big plus, but losing Tom and Connie hurt. Politics is an ugly game. Oh well, life went on.

Mountain County Sheriff's Department was always short-handed and constantly looking for good help. The big problem, however, was that the pay was horseshit. The pay for a Patrol Deputy was about half what neighboring states paid. My salary was roughly $22,000/year; simply not enough for an officer and his family to survive. I was able to because I had outside income. After working previously for 20 years, I had accumulated some assets, and had no debt, with some cash in the bank. I had created three businesses before my career as a Deputy and sold them for some gain.

But the younger guys and gals hadn't gotten to that point yet and were struggling. Both husband and wife had to work. Even in the years that I worked, all department salaries were way below standards. That was one of the things Tom fought with the Commissioners about. Bringing the pay up was paramount in order to attract good help. In many ways, it was a losing battle for Tom. It was obvious that he wanted to help us. So it was that things didn't change much in that regard. Patti had more work to do without Connie available.

Another daytime event that I initiated was a Monday morning meeting with a group of people in the lower part of the county at Johnson's Ferry. Neighborhood Watch was a very good program that brought local citizens into the equation of law enforcement. Let's face it. There simply are not enough Patrol Officers to cover a huge county. We needed help and therefore I tried to recruit the local eyes and ears to provide it.

When I first began to stop at Johnson's Ferry, the people having coffee and breakfast at the older and historic hotel there were a bit surprised. They told me that I was the first Deputy to stop and just converse with them. They were appreciative of having a Deputy do that and listen to their concerns. It isn't a large population, where most live across the bridge over the Payette river on the other side. Even though there were maybe less than a hundred people living there, they still had issues and crimes happening in the area. So I made it a habit to go there, and looked forward to arriving at 7:00 am to have breakfast with a group of about six people. Good people who enjoyed hearing about things in the department and generally discussing world events. I became one of them and they enjoyed having me.

One of the principal reasons to meet with them was to recruit them to help us control crime. We needed their help and there was no better way to do that than with local surveillance. In fact, their tips helped us nail a drug group operating from that area. It was a big deal and I thanked them profusely for their assistance. They were happy that finally their government was doing something good and constructive, as opposed to most governments and politicians that really don't give a shit about the citizens.

Neighborhood Watch was a huge aid everywhere to help the Law Enforcement Officers do their jobs. Let's face it, we're really only able to pick up the pieces after a crime. There is very little a Deputy can do to stop or prevent a crime. Only with great observation and luck would that happen.

Actually, one of our Dispatchers, Stacy, recommended that I get together with the group. Her family was the owner of the hotel/restaurant.

I tried to continue this program throughout the county with some success. I would drive down rural roads, a lot were gravel, just observing the area and stopping to talk with anyone nearby. It really didn't take a lot of time out of my daily routine to do this, and in between calls or traffic control I would venture off into little-known parts of the county and explore. Again, the people really appreciated seeing a Deputy pass their way. For me it was very satisfying.

Chapter 8
Traffic Control

When transiting from one part of the county to another, I was always observing the traffic. Idaho State Highway #55 is the main road that runs through Mountain County and is about 55 miles in length. At the southern end, the road is very curvy and meanders along the Payette River. It is simply a beautiful ride as one drives along rocky outcrops strewn with mild to medium challenging rapids. Kayakers love this stretch of the river. The mountains on each side create a semi-tunnel effect which can easily distract the driver.

Excessive speed really isn't possible nor prudent when traveling this portion of the highway. At the northern part where it meets up with Federal Highway 95, there is another canyon with a series of sharp curves and an equally beautiful river flowing along the roadway. I mention the characteristics of this highway for a reason. Because of the sharp curves of the roadway, trucks with 53-foot trailers were forbidden to pass through this route. I will explain more on this later.

Mountain County encompasses almost 3800 square miles of ranch land, four small towns, Federal forest land, wilderness area where no motorized vehicles are allowed, and many lakes and streams. It is a beautiful county and a delight to work in from the perspective of a Deputy.

However, it really taxes the Deputies because of its size and variety of terrain. Its climate in winter can also be challenging, that's why we only used SUV four-wheel drive vehicles for patrol units. We packed a lot of gear for extreme contingencies. Every day posed a new challenge. We were never bored. As explained before, the Sheriff had preeminence in the county, and as per that power, we enforced state laws everywhere in the county.

The largest town is Payette in the northern part. It straddles the beautiful Payette Lake, which is a pristine 4000-acre expanse of clear mountain water and nearly 400-feet deep. Ringed by mountains, it is a huge summer attraction for the city dwellers of Boise, Idaho. Tourists flood the town during the summer and winter provides a great landscape for snowmobiling and skiing at the nearby Brundage Mountain.

At the southern end of Mountain County's valley is the county seat of Buffalo. In between are two smaller villages. Both Payette and Buffalo have their own police force, which at times would leave their jurisdictions to back us up when needed. The law enforcement community for Mountain County was a tight one, which also included ISP officers that transited through. Several Federal Forest LEOs were included as well. We knew and trusted each other a lot. So that said we all worked together at one time or another.

During the very busy times of the summer influx of visitors, traffic control was a big issue. There were a number of long, straight stretches of highway between the southern and northern ends, which allowed drivers to push the speed limits. A very generous 65 mph limit was the posted speed for half of Highway 55 and even then I stopped countless drivers driving faster than 75.

Most of the time I had fun with the people because I really tried to give them a break and tell them to just slow it down. That was usually the case for speeds ten and lower over the limit. The effect it would have on other drivers who saw a vehicle stopped by a patrol unit with lights flashing was enough to curb their speed, for a while.

Human nature is funny. It quickly reverts to the bad habits it has established in the past, which keeps us in business. By lessening the actual speed the driver was exceeding the limit by, it helped ameliorate the bite of the fine. The fines increase with certain increments of speed. For instance, 20 miles over the limit would make a huge hurt on the pocketbook. Depending on the circumstances and attitude of the driver, my goal was to remind them with a "gentle" fine that excessive speed is a no-no.

Stops for speed ten and under were mostly for me to go "fishing". By that I mean I was looking for other more serious violations or crimes. All license plates need to have a current tab affixed to the lower right corner in the particular color for the year. It's almost impossible to see if that tab is current until we're right on top of the car or have stopped it. A 10-28 (vehicle registration check) of the license plate would give that to us quickly. A suspended driver's license was a common occurrence. That was a misdemeanor offense and could result in jail time. An outstanding warrant on the driver or a passenger would definitely mean the culprit would be visiting the Sheriff's hotel. Visible evidence in the vehicle of drugs or paraphernalia would open up a real can of worms whereupon the driver would be arrested, and the car searched and towed. But most of the time, no citation was issued with only a mild chastisement of "Please slow down and have a good rest of the day."

I rarely got angry with a driver and hammered them hard. However, one occasion sticks out in my mind about a sassy, smug little witch that was determined to yank my chain. I remember her well because her name was Lindsay, the same as my daughter's. As soon as I approached the driver's side of the car, she started in on me. I guess she was performing for the two passengers riding with her.

"Here comes the big man with a gun. Why the hell did you stop me? Was I going two miles over the limit?"

I told her in as calm and professional a voice as I could muster, the stop was for excessive speed and also that her tabs were expired. I then noticed she wasn't wearing her seatbelt. So, as I continued to explain to her the violations of traffic code she had committed, she amped up her abuse and vulgarities. I told her that such disrespect for a Law

Enforcement Officer was not earning her "brownie" points and would only cost her.

She began with remonstrations on why I shouldn't ticket her; that was a big mistake, trying to justify her actions. She was reacting like a typical spoiled brat where mommy and daddy gave her everything. All too common in our degenerate society. I told her to stay in the car and I would return shortly with her "gift", not in those words but in my mind a good proverbial "spanking".

As I said, normally I don't like to hammer a person with multiple citations, but in this case I felt it was warranted. Sometimes people are so obtuse they don't get the message until a 2 x 4 is used on them; a good old fashioned "whoopin." Something this little bitch should have had many times but never got. As the saying goes "spare the rod and spoil the child."

So that's what I gave her, not so much out of anger, but for the need of an attitude adjustment. Out of hundreds of tickets that I issued, this was the only time I gave three citations: excessive speed which doubles the fine, no seatbelt, and expired tabs. It amounted to over 200 dollars in fines and I'm sure it didn't help improve her insurance rates.

I returned to the vehicle and gave her the bad news. She wasn't pleased, but her demeanor and mouth had noticeably changed. She spun her tires as she left and I only shook my head in disgust but I said to myself "YES". That time it felt good to hand out retribution for stupidity. As the saying goes, "Stupidity should hurt."

This incident shows the wide gap of what a Deputy experiences. The aforementioned case of the birthday boy and this one exemplify what a Deputy sees when dealing with the public. The birthday boy was contrite and humble in his pleading, whereas Lindsay was just the opposite.

Our job is to get people to embrace compliance with the law. It's for everyone's good. A safe, orderly, and peaceful society is reliant on those that oversee it. Without honest and just oversight, a society disintegrates into chaos, which we are seeing in most major cities. Poor education, poverty, and unjust police and courts are endemic in all of our large cities. It is a vicious downward spiral of collapse that will end in anarchy.

Where a citizenry is poorly educated, witnesses rampant double standards in the court system, and there is abusive police action, the end result is explosive. I would no more want to work in a large city than to fight in a war zone, because that's what they are; war zones. Murders, violent gangs, bum rush store thefts, where organized groups rush into a store and steal, riots were not the kind of law enforcement I wanted. I much preferred a small rural county where life is much more subdued. Don't get me wrong. We saw crime of all levels, just at a greatly reduced proportion.

At the opposite end of the spectrum, traffic stops can be fun.

One day, I was patrolling along the perimeter road around Lake Payette, which led to many lake homes. Even though there were not a lot of homes next to this portion of the road, the speed limit was posted at 25 mph. For me it was ridiculously slow and I considered 35 mph to be a reasonable limit. So, if I made a stop, I made 35 my guideline in judging a vehicle's radared speed.

As I was returning back to the town of Payette, I noticed a van approaching at a speed of about 45 mph, and my radar confirmed what I observed. I immediately turned around and stopped the van and radioed in my 10-20 (location) with the plate number and vehicle description. Being it was daytime and the type of vehicle was normally of a family, I approached with a more relaxed manner. Upon arriving at the driver's side door I saw two couples of medium age and a woman driving. I suddenly realized who I had stopped.

The male in the passenger seat was none other than the U.S. Senator from Idaho, Dirk Kempthorne. *Oh, boy*, I thought. *How do I handle this one?*

It came quickly to me that I could have some fun with them. I, of course, asked for the driver's license, proof of insurance and registration, and commented,

"I would have had to stop the wife of our Senator, right?"

Senator Kempthorne simply smiled and said yes. The couple in the back seat were enjoying it immensely. I'm sure they wanted to see how I handled the situation. I told them I would be back and returned to my patrol unit and radioed in the information.

The conversation went like this:

"Buffalo 2114."

"2114" was the reply.

"10-27 on last of, get this, Kempthorne, and first of Patricia," I normally didn't inject words like "get this" in my communication with Dispatch, but I couldn't resist. I'm sure the Dispatcher, Vic, was just as surprised with the person I had stopped. Everybody knew the Kempthornes.

While waiting on Dispatch to come back, I decided to have fun with the occupants of the car. Sergeant Joe had taught me a trick to use on special occasions and I put it into play. I took my business card and wrote on the back: "In lieu of a $56 fine, you promise to take your husband out to supper at a nice restaurant for this amount or more." After completing my substitute citation, Dispatch came back with the all clear. I replied "10-4" and returned to the van.

I gave Mrs. Kempthorne her documents back and explained that I was giving her a citation of a different sort. I asked her to read out loud what I had written on the back of my card and to agree to the stipulations. She did and I told her to hand the card to her husband, Dirk, who could redeem it at the time of his choosing.

By this time, the couple in the back were laughing heartily and Senator Kempthorne was smiling broadly. I wished them a fine remainder of the day and cautioned her to be mindful of the speed limit. I hoped they all left with a favorable attitude of the Mountain County Sheriff's Department.

Now, one might ask if I showed favoritism to her because of her status and the answer would be absolutely not. Even though the speed limit was a posted 25 mph, 35 mph was more reasonable. My guideline of ten over that speed was the reason I stopped her at 20 over the posted limit. Most of my stops at ten over were mainly to look for other infractions and if all was well, I would send the driver on their way with a friendly chastisement.

That's what this stop amounted to, although I never knew if she fulfilled her part of the bargain. Anyway, it was an example of making the job fun.

I issued many citations to drivers who violated the traffic code and I only had one that was rejected by the Court.

The traffic code of Idaho for excessive speed included a clause of "reasonable and prudent." What does that mean? Speed limits were established on roadways according to the conditions of that roadway. A standard of 25 mph to 65 mph was the range in Mountain County. Most of my traffic work was on the main highway that ran through the county. Sometimes weather conditions extant on Highway 55 precluded the ability to drive at the posted limit. Fog, ice, heavy snow, or rain are factors that would fall under the "reasonable and prudent" clause. They create conditions on the roadway that prevent a vehicle from driving at the normal speed limit. It was just common sense not to drive fast in those conditions.

With that in mind, I was driving north one evening on Highway 55 under snowy and icy conditions where I could drive at only 45 mph in a 65 mph zone, in a four-wheel drive with a visibility of maybe 30 feet. It was nasty. Suddenly, a vehicle came the opposite direction at 60 mph, recorded by my radar, in those conditions.

Although I had never issued a citation under the reasonable and prudent clause, I felt this one was a warranted time. To me it was plain "loco" to be going that fast with very poor visibility. It was an exigency ripe for disaster. So I turned on my overhead lights, waited until it was safe to turn, and finally stopped the vehicle a half a mile farther on. I radioed in my position to Dispatch along with my pertinent information, and cautiously approached the vehicle on the passenger's side.

There was no way I was going to stand in the roadway waiting for another vehicle to hit me. I would do that occasionally, even though the conditions were good but with heavy traffic. One never knows what an inattentive driver will do. It was a procedure of good officer safety. I wanted to go home after my shift in one piece.

The driver rolled down the window and of course asked why I stopped him. I explained, "Look, you were driving way too fast for these conditions."

He protested, "But I was driving under the speed limit."

I explained to him that his speed was 60, which was way too fast for the conditions. I told him I would be back shortly after receiving his documents. After Dispatch came back with an all clear, I wrote the citation under the clause mentioned. In my notes I recorded the conditions extant at the time. I returned to the vehicle and explained the citation to him. Of course, he protested, and I, being a wonderful human being, told him that he could contest the citation in Court. I elaborated that he might be successful in reversing the charge.

He took my advice and truly was successful in overturning it. I suspect the courts don't want to mess with this part of the code. I imagine they felt it too subjective and hard to substantiate. Oh, well, I tried and really didn't have another opportunity to use the "reasonable and prudent" clause again.

As I explained about the nature of Mountain County's main roadway, State Highway 55, it had canyons on both ends with very curvy sections. They were of such a condition that a semi-truck hauling a 53-foot trailer simply couldn't transit without the trailer crossing over into the oncoming lane. The highway, therefore, was restricted to trailers no more than 48-feet.

Early on in my career with the department, I realized that many 53-footers were disregarding the warning signs at both ends and risking huge fines by taking this shortcut north and south. The longer legal route, U.S. Highway 95 took another half hour to transit.

My ISP friend Tim mentioned this to me and suggested I come up to speed on stopping these trucks. So I figured "why not?" I studied the law and what procedure was proper after making a stop of these long trucks. I found out that the fine was about $250 plus the added expense of hiring a lead guide car with lights to get back to the legal route. It was very expensive for any driver who chanced going through the county illegally; in addition to the time wasted waiting for me to handle the matter.

A lot of times I called an ISP officer to do a thorough inspection under USDOT regulations if I felt the log books weren't current or the loading of the trailer was wrong. Regardless, it cost the driver and the company a huge amount of time and expense, but I felt it was justified since it kept those trucks from endangering other traffic in the canyons.

Over the time as a Deputy in Mountain County, I made numerous stops of 53-footers and started a trend with the other Deputies. I will note that with each citation we issued, part of the fine went into the county coffers. Although the amount from these citations wasn't great, because most went to the courts and state, it was still something. So there was a double incentive to control traffic of all sorts.

I know, some might ask if we had quotas to fulfill, and the answer is a resounding no. Our job was not about issuing citations, but encompassed a lot more than just traffic. Traffic control took up maybe 30 percent of my time. It was an adjunct to our main responsibilities. So, there was never any mention of quotas in the department.

Interestingly enough, Dispatch one day called me to report an accident between one such tractor trailer and car at the southern end of the county. All traffic was blocked, so I and a reserve officer accompanying me raced down with lights and siren some 20 miles away. It was in the middle of the day and there was a fair amount of traffic to get around.

Sometimes drivers were slow getting out of our way until we got right up on them and they finally noticed an emergency vehicle on their tail "screaming" at them. I could vary the type of siren used, which would help break a driver's fixation on the road ahead; as I said before people just don't check their rearview mirrors enough. Then, suddenly they're shocked to see me on their butt and broke hard and swerved to the side of the road to let me pass.

On this run, we came upon a black Suburban that simply wouldn't yield. I saw the driver look in his mirror and continue on as if he owned the road. I couldn't get around him because of oncoming traffic and when I finally could pass, I told my Reserve Deputy to motion him to properly yield, but to no avail. I was furious but I continued on to the accident scene. This was the only time as a Deputy that I was that angry and determined to arrest the driver for failure to yield, which was a misdemeanor. When I arrived, I explained to my Lieutenant who was on scene what had happened.

When the Suburban came shortly thereafter I motioned for him to pull over to the side of the road, which he did. I and the Lieutenant approached the car and the driver wanted to know why I stopped him. I asked him if he knew what to do when an emergency vehicle approached him from behind with lights and siren.

He said he did to which I asked, "Why then didn't you pull to the side of the road and stop?"

He replied, "I didn't need to. You had plenty of room to get around me."

That answer made me so angry that I wanted to arrest him on the spot. However, I asked to see his license, registration, and proof of insurance, and told him I would be issuing a citation for failure to yield. It was obvious to him and my Lieutenant that I was very agitated about the whole event. He came back with the smartass remark, "You're the big man with the gun. What, are you going to shoot me?" Oh, boy, that really "tripped my trigger", and were it not for my Lieutenant coaching me away from the bastard, I probably would have.

We went to my patrol unit and I radioed in the driver's information. My Lieutenant recognized him as some big shot businessman from Boise. He worked on calming me down by saying, "Look, I know the guy's an asshole and deserves a citation, but you're angry and that's not a good time to issue one. We'll go back and settle this down and give him a warning."

I agreed and did calm down enough to go back to the vehicle. We slowly walked back and I calmly told this prick that I was not going to issue him a citation after all. I simply gave him his documents back and walked away. I did hear my Lieutenant tell the guy, "You're lucky, you could have gone to jail for your actions." With no comment from the man, he drove away.

I suddenly realized we had more important things to do managing traffic around the accident scene. No one was really hurt, but the car lodged under the trailer was history. It just exemplifies what could happen when those long, 53-foot trailers cross over into the other lane. In some spots on this curvy canyon road, it was either collide with rock walls of the canyon, or go into the river alongside if a trailer was in one's lane. I'm sure there was a big insurance claim on the part of the harmed party. Oh, well, stupidity should hurt.

On the ride back to the office, my reserve officer and I spoke at length about what we went through. He learned a lot and we began to laugh and relieve the tension from the occasion. Tom rode with me occasionally when he wasn't working at his regular job, and was part of another big escapade later on. He eventually hired on as a full time Deputy.

Sometimes a Deputy has the chance to have a lot of enjoyment from a traffic stop. One such time for me occurred when I stopped a car going too fast entering the northern side of Buffalo. I turned around, turned on my overhead lights, and the car stopped. After I radioed in the particulars, I approached the car.

Now, it happened to be the middle of the day and there was a fair amount of traffic going to and fro. An older overweight woman rolled down her window and kindly said, "Hello ,officer, was I doing something wrong?"

I explained that she was going a little fast as she entered

town and asked her for her documents. I told her that I would be right back and for her to stay in the car. I found no problems with her report from Dispatch and returned to give her documents back. I explained that I wasn't going to give her a ticket and cautioned her to slow down in this part of the highway. Again the State had posted it at 25 mph when it should've been 35. I said, "You have a nice rest of your day."

As I started to retreat, she quizzically looked at me and blurted out, "Aren't you going to give me a ticket?"

I replied, "No ma'am, I just wanted you to be aware of the speed zone and slow down."

Suddenly she unbuckled her seatbelt, opened her door, and jumped out to give me a big bear hug. I was totally taken aback but pleasantly surprised at her embrace. She exclaimed, "Thank you so much. I'm going to tell all of my friends about you."

At the moment this happened, another Buffalo police car passed and saw what happened. It wasn't long before all of the law enforcement community knew about the incident. I was famous, for a while. The next time I entered the Sheriff's Department, someone jokingly commented about my officer safety.

I quickly responded, "Yeah, I was embraced by Ma Barker herself." We all laughed about it.

Events like this are what make the job fun. Later on, as I patrolled around Buffalo and talked to people, they all knew about the "big hug". But that was what my philosophy of law enforcement was all about. Engender affiliation with the Deputies of Mountain County.

Part of our duties early on was to test drivers who were trying to obtain their driver's license. It was later turned over to a contracted company to do the actual behind the wheel tests. Deputies were assigned to give those driving tests.

One day, I was given the assignment to test an older gentleman who had gone through some difficult medical problems. His doctor gave the ok to test him in actual behind the wheel driving. So someone drove him in his car to the Sheriff's office to be tested. The man was well into his eighties but seemed to be fairly cognitive.

With my list of driving requirements, we entered the car and began the test. I buckled my seatbelt but he failed to buckle his. I told him to do it; one strike. I told him to back the car and proceed down the street, which he did.

But then the errors began. I told him to turn left at a certain street, which he did, but forgetting to signal. Throughout the test he committed many other mistakes. I felt that he was not capable of handling the car safely. At one point, I had to tell him to brake immediately.

I ended the test prematurely. I knew he was not capable of driving a vehicle safely any more. Upon returning to the Sheriff's Office, I explained to him and his daughter that I could not certify him to drive. His sad look almost crushed me. I knew I had just taken this man's freedom away. I almost cried.

Our job was sometimes very difficult. We represented the law of the County of Mountain and the State of Idaho, and sometimes that plain sucked! This poor man was now being limited by the powers invested in me, and I hurt for him. As I grow older, I know that fate awaits me as well.

Last to mention was my traffic stop into "continuing education." I was working a night shift and while entering the north side of Buffalo, I confirmed by radar a car leaving at 15 mph over the limit. So, naturally I turned and stopped the vehicle.

Upon reaching the driver's side window it was opened only sufficiently to pass the driver's documents. That was a first. I asked him to roll down the window so that I could see him and talk to him. I, as always, wanted to see inside for my safety and insisted that he comply.

However, he wouldn't. So I backed away and called for backup. After an ISP officer arrived, I went back to the vehicle and reiterated for the driver to roll down the window, and if he didn't, I would arrest him for obstruction; he complied.

His wife in the passenger side began to argue about my method and wanted my name. She shouted that they could sue me.That got my attention because no Deputy wants to confront that possibility. My demeanor softened and I explained the reason for the stop. To make the story short, I issued a citation for speed and let them move on. I pow wowed with my backup officer and he also thought the incident was strange.

The next day, when I came on shift, I was met by the Sheriff and the County Attorney. They had received a complaint from the driver I stopped and told me that he was not a happy camper and wanted to sue.

The CA told me he placated the man by canceling the citation and that he would "advance" my education. It turned out that the driver was an attorney and was doing what was legal. He told me that the thing I should have done differently was to explain to him that I needed him to roll down the window so as to be able to identify him as the person on his driver's license. That was the way I needed to phrase my order.

"Ok, that makes sense," I said, and because this was such an important point, this subtlety of a correct approach to a Fourth Amendment detention was also explained to the rest of the Deputies.

The job of a County Attorney is not only to prosecute cases but also to keep all LEOs in the county to stay on the straight and narrow to avoid lawsuits. If a Deputy is sued, that lawsuit goes all the way up to the county. This event began to awaken me to that possibility and the knowledge that if I screwed up, I could lose everything. I saw the handwriting on the wall.

Chapter 9
Under Arrest

When a person is placed under arrest, it is an act of taking away their freedom. It is not a pleasant event for the detainee, and if a Deputy is to be really honest, for them neither. It involves a lot of emotion for the person arrested and potential danger to the officer. Most of the time, we radioed Dispatch for backup and before the arrest was effected, that assisting officer was on scene. It was imperative to deescalate the situation to the point where the person was cooperative with the instructions of the Deputy. That involved good psychology, calm demeanor, and respect for the offender. It was vital to avoid a fight for both officer and arrestee in order to prevent injuries.

My personal approach to any arrest went as follows: "Look, we have a problem here and it needs to be fixed. Let's go to Buffalo and do that. There is no other way."

Most of the time when I said it like that, I could literally see the person relax and put their hands behind their back so I could easily place the handcuffs on their wrists.

Why? Could the reader see the psychology used? Well, in that manner I didn't isolate them. I didn't make it adversarial. I used the words "we," and "let's," which included me in the equation. I became their advocate with the desire to help them and correct the problem. It was not my job to incriminate nor judge the person. That was the job of the County Attorney and Court. And remember always, a person is innocent until proven guilty.

So, as a Deputy we must be mindful to treat the arrested person with respect and kindness, if possible.

In the end I hoped that I had gained someone who had no animus for me in the exercising of my duties. It goes back to my mantra of "Humility is the catalyst that makes power benevolent." Humility doesn't mean weakness but rather an understanding of what and who we really are. It comes from the Latin word *humus*, which means dirt or earth. The substance from which God made us.

Power was given to us by the Sheriff, who was given it by the people. Of and by ourselves we had no authority and were behest with it under the condition to exercise it wisely and justly. I believed in "Treating others as I wanted to be treated." The Golden Rule is too often overlooked or forgotten when dealing with our fellow man.

Often, when someone asked me about an action they were considering, whether it was good or bad, I simply asked them if they would want it done to them. If no, then don't do it to others, period.

When a citizen breaks the law, it is our job to bring the

person to the authority that will decide the corrective action. To criticize, berate, and anger a person under detention is stupid and counterproductive. It only worsens the problem.

One can see how in the inner cities of America there is so much hatred for any authority. The chain of abuses perpetrated on the citizens living in the impoverished areas has fomented great antipathy and distrust of the police. That's tragic! It was my job to avoid that at all costs and to foster an amity for the Mountain County Sheriff's Department.

Making an arrest in the case of a traffic stop is an involved procedure. After handcuffing a person, the process is the same whether from a vehicle or other locations. I would lean the person against the car or a wall to stabilize their stance. I would spread their feet and begin the search of their body.

I would first ask, "Do you have anything on you that could poke me, cut me, or make me bleed?" Depending on their answer, I would start by removing any head covering and search the head hairs. I would then proceed down the body to the waist area and feel around the belt or waist strap of any type to see if any potential knife or sharp instrument was hidden in the waist area. From there I proceeded down the back of the legs and with both hands, I would feel the entire leg area down to the ankles and shoes.

This would mean that I would touch their crotch area, which is an excellent hiding place, with the back of my hand.

Now, with women it became a more sensitive subject. In the breast area, it was mandatory to search the bra and around the breast with the back of my hand to feel if they had hidden anything in their bra. I can only say that this was always a difficult moment in searching a woman's body, as well as the crotch area. I know that one might think it an opportunity to take advantage of the situation, however that never was the case for me.

An example of why a total and complete search of anyone's body is vital happened while I was in P.O.S.T. training. We had to search a woman completely for any contraband or weapons. We all made the mistake of not fully searching this person's breast area. That mistake cost us all our lives, figuratively not literally.

When we finished and removed the cuffs, she pulled a derringer from her bra and shot us. Although it is not a high probability that such a thing could occur, it is a fact that some practiced women can slip their handcuffs and escape or harm the officer.

If possible, we would ask for a female officer to handle the task. Usually they don't have any compunction about "feeling up" another of their sex. Officer safety is the primary concern, along with removing and bagging what they have on them, including things in the pockets, as well as bracelets, necklaces, and wallets. It all gets bagged and cataloged.

I'd even take off any spiked heeled shoes which a woman

could stick through the wire cage separating us in the patrol unit.

After the body search was completed I would inform them of their rights. **"You have the right to remain silent. Anything you say can and will be used against you in a court of law. You have the right to talk to a lawyer for advice before we ask you any questions. You have the right to have a lawyer with you during questioning. If you cannot afford a lawyer, one will be appointed for you before any questioning if you wish. If you decide to answer questions now without a lawyer present, you have the right to stop answering at any time."**

I would ask if the person understood what I just read or verbalized to them. If they answered yes then we were good to go, if not, I explained in a simple way to just keep their mouth shut. Even the dumbest understood that. They were then placed in the back seat on a "comfortable" plastic seat designed to accommodate a person with their hands behind their backs.

Many times, while in the back seat a detainee would just start talking and admit to things they shouldn't have. This is called "excited utterance," which is perfectly admissible in court. They were warned previously via the Miranda explanation, but some simply couldn't control their emotions nor mouth.

Phase one completed, I would begin to search the car during a traffic stop. This was necessary because the car needed to be towed, or, if there was a capable driver, then that person could take the car. By this time I would have requested that Dispatch send a tow truck.

Later on I will relate a story of my biggest "bust," where the arrestee didn't want his truck towed.

We would wait until the tow truck arrived and had taken the vehicle to the impound lot before leaving the scene and bringing the prisoner to the Mountain County Jail. Now, all of my stops and arrests were recorded by my audio cassette unit in my front left pocket. At the time we did not have cameras in the patrol unit nor on our uniforms. It was strictly via an audio cassette recorder that we recorded our conversations. In today's standards, that would be like using a "Dirty Harry" revolver instead of my Glock 40 with 16 rounds. Obviously a bit outdated but still effective.

We then proceeded to the jail where, via camera, the jail administration would open a door to permit my patrol unit to enter. One or several jailers would meet me to assist in exiting the prisoner from my vehicle and bring them into the secured jail area. I would gather all the belongings of the person and my paperwork and follow. From that point, the detainee was in the hands of the jail personnel and I would explain the charges to the staff so they could complete the booking process. Only rarely would I have to fingerprint the person in case the jail staff was shorthanded or busy elsewhere. But fingerprinting was part of our training and job as well.

Now, an exception to this procedure was when I arrested a person for DUI. I would bring the person to a special room where I would administer a breathalyzer test. This had to occur first in order to determine the amount of alcohol in the blood. We were required to test twice and the machine would emit a paper showing the results. If it was established that the reading showed .08 B.A.C. (blood alcohol content) or above, then that was what was needed to incarcerate the subject. From there we would go to booking.

With that completed, I would usually go into the Dispatch Center and sit, drink some coffee, and generally "depressurize." It was fun to talk with Vic, Laurie, or Tracy and discuss the events of the day; mostly small talk but an escape from what I just had to do.

Arresting someone was stressful for both involved, and generally the person was out the next day on bail. However, the days ahead for such a person were expensive and convulsive for the whole family.

Our team of Dispatchers were excellent at their jobs, and sometimes they would correct me on my radio protocol. That suited me just fine, since I only wanted to make their jobs easier.

Tracy was related to the family in Johnson's Ferry that owned the old hotel and would discuss what people were saying about my meeting with them. I'm happy to say there were no negative comments. According to her, they appreciated me going there and just hanging out with them for a while. One picks up a lot of gossip in a group like that and sometimes leads to an interesting end; as I spoke of before.

Laurie was the wife of one of the Payette Police Officers and Vic later married Sergeant Bill and went on to become an ISP officer. All in all, it was a pretty tight group of people bonded together by a common theme; law enforcement. I've lost track of everyone in the department since I left and retired years later.

In my years as a Deputy Sheriff, I made many arrests of various kinds: domestic violence, attempted murder, drugs, but mostly drunk driving.

Probably the most dangerous situation where an arrest results is involving a domestic violence occurrence. We were trained not to go into a volatile domestic call alone. These were very dangerous. Most of the time the woman calls in for help from an abusive husband or partner and when the decision is made to arrest the man, the woman would fight the officers to not arrest him.

It is absolutely a weird dichotomy of thinking, opposing thoughts, when she wants help but will fight to keep us from helping her. It is almost a Stockholm Syndrome situation where a captive has been so affected and brainwashed that they identify and sympathize with their captor. Perhaps fear of being alone is a big part, but regardless we always handled such calls with a minimum of two officers.

Of course alcohol was usually a big part of the mess and would blur the cognitive ability of the two involved. We would always separate them and take them to different parts of the house or location, where they couldn't hear or interact with each other.

Invariably, I would handcuff the acclaimed assailant before investigating what the hell happened. I use the word hell because generally they were living in a hell they created. It was always difficult figuring out who the real culprit was, even though one or both might be bloodied. In our society, people generally assume that the male is the assailant and the female the victim. However, that is not always the case. For instance, in one of my arrests I arrested the wife.

The husband actually called Dispatch 911 seeking help. When we arrived at the rundown filthy house, the man was outside waiting, with a nice-sized lump on his head. My partner was given the responsibility of interviewing the husband and I went in the house, cautiously, to find the wife.

She was in the kitchen with crying children nearby also waiting. I placed her under "protective custody" by handcuffing her and explained to her that she was not under arrest but custodial care to prevent injury to me and her.

I called Dispatch to have a person from Social Services, Child Protective Services in other states, to look after the children. Seeing the conditions of the children and house, I felt it warranted. I then began my "inquisition" on what happened.

She was pretty emotional and used language I won't repeat here. In essence, he was a lazy, do nothing, drunk from whom she couldn't get any help. Her frustration boiled over to violence when she clobbered him with a heavy-duty cast iron fry pan.

I found that women love those pans; they're heavy, within reach, and have the same effect as a 2 x 4. Great attention-getters. In some cases, big kitchen knives worked as well, only with greater bloodletting. Ambulances were needed in those cases.

Anyway, she basically detailed her story and I decided she needed to go to jail. So I told her so and she, of course paradoxically, worried about the children. From what I witnessed, there didn't seem to be much concern provided to the children before. I told her that Social Services would care for them.

After placing her in my patrol unit, I discussed the situation with my partner. He confirmed pretty much what I had heard from the wife and said he would monitor the situation until S.S. arrived and determined what was to be done with the children. In this case, they were taken to a care home for their safety until the court decided what to do with them. The husband was not someone responsible enough with whom to leave the children; that was obvious to us both.

Unfortunately, domestic violence calls were very common, and as our society continues to degenerate, they are becoming more numerous and violent.

As explained, for any Deputy, it was the most dangerous event we could face and for that reason, a minimum of two officers were needed. We couldn't risk being a victim as well. People striking out in frustration, anger, and desperation were always factors considered. So, during such confrontations, our antennas were up and "wiggling."

What affected me the most was the hurt experienced by the children. They always suffered and would carry those feelings and memories for the rest of their lives. That is the tragedy of a broken home and society; the children always pay the heavier price.

Sometimes justice comes late. That was the case with an arrest I made of a senior citizen.

Idaho had just passed a law regarding domestic abuse that made it a felony if blood or bruising was evident on the victim. I was the first officer in the county or even perhaps the state to arrest someone under that law.

I was dispatched to the Payette City Police Station to handle the complaint. The officer, Cecile, explained that the victim didn't live in the city but in the county which was our jurisdiction. So I found that an older woman and her daughter were there and had already filed a complaint of abuse against the senior woman's husband. The abuse had gone on for years and the daughter finally got her mother to come in.

I could clearly see the fear in the woman's face. She was terrified of the possible repercussions of the charge. Evidently, the husband was a very controlling bastard and they fooled him to bring them to town to shop. I interrogated them both about the current event and the history of the abuse. I shook my head in disbelief at the story they told.

The daughter was fully aware of her father's abuse and told me it took her a long time to get her mother to proceed with a complaint. The woman's fear was palpable. I then asked the woman to show me any wounds or bruises, which she did.

The case had just transited from a misdemeanor to a felony under the new law. I took photos of the bruises and finished up with my questioning. I asked them where the husband might be and the make and model of car he was driving. My intent was to go look for and arrest him. I closed out my meeting with the women, thanked Cecile for her help, and radioed Dispatch my intent.

It was easy for me because, as I was leaving the Police Station, the daughter whispered to me, "That's him," as a car drove into the parking lot. I told the women to stay inside and then approached the car.

I noticed an old, white-haired man exit the vehicle and walk toward me. I stopped him and asked him his name. He confirmed that he was the suspect of the charge.

I said, "Please turn around and put your hands behind your back, I'm placing you under arrest."

Although he complied, he was greatly confused and pleaded, "Why are you arresting me? What have I done?"

I informed him that I was arresting him for domestic violence under the new state statute, and that I was charging him with a felony. He had no more comments from then on until the Sheriff's Department. He was smart enough to keep his mouth shut.

From that point on I was never called to court nor appraised of the outcome. I'm sure a plea deal was reached and no jail time dished out. He was in his eighties and not in good health and probably would have died in prison.

I say prison because all felons went to the state penitentiary in Boise. Our jail was not set up to hold a felon nor incarcerate someone for more than a year. So I imagine a fine was levied and great supervision imposed to protect the wife and daughter from retribution.

It shouldn't have taken so long to stop the violence against this woman. I gave my thoughts about it earlier and know that fear and loneliness are debilitating emotions, which forestall a weaker woman from taking action. I thank the strength of the daughter to end this madness.

To quote the Bible, "Justice not speedily executed, the heart of the people is fully set to do evil." That was the case here and throughout our society for all crime. Albeit late, justice was finally meted out.

I write later about my "acquaintance" from San Quentin State Prison whom we dealt with on an illegal gun charge. He really wasn't a bad guy on a superficial level, but one usually doesn't spend time in California's oldest and perhaps toughest prison by not being culpable. He did kill a man out of anger in a bar fight, which earned him the passage there.

Although I didn't know who I was pursuing down a side road for speeding, it became evident that he didn't want to stop. I saw that he was headed for his house and I let him get there before I detained him.

When I approached his pickup, I recognized who I had stopped; John the paroled felon. It was patently evident that he had been drinking, first from the strong odor of alcoholic drink emanating from the vehicle, and second because I quickly noticed a large, partially-consumed bottle of bourbon on the passenger side floor. I asked him if he had been drinking and he replied caustically, "Of course, you're not blind, are you?"

Knowing I potentially had a fighter on my hands, I tried to remain calm and pleasant, got his documents, and told him to stay in the pickup.

Upon sitting in my patrol unit, I immediately radioed Dispatch with the information and requested backup. By the information I gave them, Dispatch knew as well whom I had stopped.

Not waiting for backup, I returned to John's truck and asked him to step out so I could perform sobriety tests. He was immediately testy with me and said, "This is bullshit. I'm not doing anything. If you are going to arrest me, then do it. Quit fucking around with me."

He had assumed a fighting stance and I overcame it by simply replying, "Look, we have a problem here. Let's get it resolved. I know you could probably beat the crap out of me, but that will only make a bad situation far worse. So, let's go to Buffalo and get it fixed."

By not isolating him and not treating him with an arrogant and condescending demeanor, he began to realize I was right.

He lowered his arms, put them behind his back, and said, "Ok, let's do this."

I handcuffed him and knew I had just avoided a nasty fight.

By this time, a backup Deputy finally arrived and we handled the processing of evidence, the open bottle in the pickup, and inspection of the vehicle and an accounting of his personal items. We did not tow the vehicle because it was safely parked at his home. I radioed that I had one in custody and would be heading their way.

On the drive to the Sheriff's Department, we had a very interesting conversation. John started it by saying, "Thanks for not treating me like shit. Most cops are assholes but you're not one of them."

I explained to him my philosophy about treating all my detainees with respect and not judging them. My job was only to bring a citizen to the place that will judge and decide punishment. I even told him a little about my errant past. I then asked him what had happened that put him in San Quentin. He opened up about the event in a bar fight that resulted in him killing the man. He claimed that it was just another bar fight that resulted in death. He said his life in prison was a constant battle with other inmates and he always had to be alert. He didn't want to go back.

A message I have for other LEOs. You get more with honey than you do with vinegar, so treat people with respect. Law enforcement in general is garnering a very bad reputation for improper use of force and mistreatment of people. More and more we are hearing such reports in the news and it is alienating whole populations of people.

Unfortunately, we are seeing in America the corruption of what were once highly-respected institutions: the FBI and the DOJ (Department of Justice). The citizens are clearly seeing double standards in the application of law from both, and that is very foreboding. This must stop or our great nation will deteriorate into tyranny.

Chapter 10
Notable Events

As a Deputy for the Mountain County Sheriff I, like all LEOs, have experienced many situations which merit relating in a book such as this one; most that are tragic, sad, ugly, but also other that are humorous. This chapter is devoted to telling those stories which, when related verbally to many acquaintances, these have said, "You need to write a book."

Most people have no idea what a Deputy or any other LEO goes through. They think they know by watching many cop shows on television or film but don't understand that most of those films or programs aren't real or accurate. They are purely Hollywood embellishments of what we go through. A good example of this is the long-running series "Gunsmoke," which, at the start of each episode Marshal Matt Dillon faced off against a bad guy in the street and killed the miscreant with his fast and accurate draw. One bullet was all that was needed. I can only say that was a load of bullshit, as is so much of what the film industry portrays.

Any LEO will confirm that when the lead starts flying, they are not going to expose themselves in the open. Cover and concealment are the key words. A well-trained Deputy is looking for protection against such danger, even with the bulletproof vest one wears. You might recall a famous shootout in North Hollywood in February 1997, where two heavily armed bank robbers took on the police. Almost 2000 rounds were fired between the robbers and police. The bad guys were firing rifle rounds and the police only had 9 millimeter bullets from their pistols. After seeing the video of the gunfight from NBC News, one could see that the assailants were walking around with impunity covered with body armor shooting at the cowering police officers.

Nobody was standing out in the open like Matt Dillon challenging the robbers. All the policemen were hunkered down behind their squad cars or other defensive positions. Actually, even with bulletproof vests, a rifle round could easily penetrate the vest and injure or kill the officer. Those officers knew what they were facing and did all they could to stay alive knowing they were insufficiently armed. A 9 millimeter weapon is virtually worthless in a gunfight. Compared to a .40 or .45 caliber arm, a 9 mm only punches holes and has little stopping power. A lot of Federal and State agencies have switched over to these more potent weapons because of their stopping power. A .45 caliber bullet is tops for knock-down power but such a weapon has less bullets in the magazine. Whereas a .40 caliber has almost equal power with more cartridges available.

As mentioned earlier, my duty weapon was a Glock 22–.40 caliber, which fit my hand well with 16 rounds; one chambered. The end result of the North Hollywood firefight was twelve officers and eight bystanders injured and the two suspects dead.

The point of this narrative is the life of a Deputy or any LEO varies greatly from what one sees through a Hollywood lens. We want to go home at the end of the day healthy, and standing out in the open to face down an assailant with a gun is a no-no. With that in mind, the following anecdotal stories picture what we as Deputies experienced in dealing with the public, although varied in many ways according to what each Deputy encountered.

Earlier I mentioned my disdain for the "Federales" who thought themselves superior in training and education. I found out early in my time as a Deputy that such arrogance was an illusion. One day the Sheriff assigned me and my Lieutenant to assist a team of BATF (Bureau of Alcohol, Tobacco and Firearms) agents investigating a paroled felon who supposedly had an illegal weapon. This felon, of whom I wrote earlier, by law was not permitted to have guns. This male felon was a "graduate" from the famous San Quentin state prison in California. As I related, he was paroled after ten years for a manslaughter charge after killing a man in a bar fight. He was living with his wife in one of the smaller towns in the county. Of course someone tipped off the BATF that he was in possession and three agents, led by a woman, came to investigate.

Before entering the property, we discussed how to handle the situation. The agents strapped on their sidearms carried low on the leg like a gunfighter and adorned themselves with bulletproof vests with the **BATF** acronym on the back. Every day we went to work, we were outfitted properly all the time of our shift, with our vests under our duty shirt. My Lieutenant and I looked at each other and rolled our eyes. The pretentiousness of most Federal agents is excessive. So we proceeded to walk down the driveway to the house and were met by the wife of this man.

Now, to add to this scenario, a warrant was not needed to search the felon nor his home. His rights were abrogated when he entered prison and was released on parole. The lead agent explained this to the wife, who was a bit agitated, and she became more so when told that her husband might go back to prison.

Now comes the moment of disgust for both of us Deputies. This lead woman agent didn't seem to have much knowledge about officer safety. She was speaking to the wife with her gun exposed to the wife and unprotected. In the state of agitation in which she was, the spouse could easily have grabbed the agent's pistol and started shooting.

As I have explained, officer safety is paramount in meeting with the public, especially in controversial encounters. This agent was oblivious to such concerns and as a result endangered all of us. My Lieutenant and I looked at each other and we moved apart and backed away ten feet. The others didn't even notice our defensive moves. If something happened, we were ready.

Fortunately nothing did develop other than our entering the house, where a shotgun was recovered. The paroled felon argued that it wasn't his and that he didn't know it was there. The wife said it was hers and she had put it in a safe place. Regardless, it was a minor violation of his parole terms and the shotgun was taken by the BATF agents, however he was not arrested.

In summation of what we witnessed, we were not impressed with this group of Federal LEOs. I did work with other Federal agents who were National Forest officers and were out in the forests regularly. They dressed just like us because they were constantly working their bailiwicks as well. I considered them professionals and nothing like the ones of whom I just wrote.

A preventable death is always a tragedy. It's not possible to erase from one's memory the sight of such a useless ending to another's life. Such was what happened one night while on a night shift. My expertise during these dark hours was stopping and arresting drunk drivers and as it so happened I knew of an individual who often drove home drunk after visiting his favorite bar in one of the small towns. It was around 10:30 pm that fateful night when I was passing by this bar observing that the person's pickup was parked outside. Now, it was not my nor the Sheriff's policy to sit on any bar or restaurant to try and catch a drunk. That was bad for the establishment's business and really not ethical. However, during my coming and going throughout the area, I would observe whether that vehicle was still parked.

Then I received a Dispatch call to assist and backup two Payette City officers handling a party of students who had been drinking alcoholic beverages. So I proceeded to the location code 2 some fifteen miles away and arrived at the home I knew was that of the Superintendent of Schools for the district. I wondered why there was a party going on so late, and if maybe it was for noise of frivolity only.

Well, I found out shortly, as I entered the home, that that was not only the case. The seventeen-year-old daughter of the parents, whom were away on a trip for some education seminar, had decided to take advantage of the situation and throw a party for her friends. As I entered, one of the girls exclaimed, "Oh, no Lindsay's dad is here."

I chuckled and recognized many of the youths present; my daughter's friends. At this time she was away on a student exchange program in Japan. She had studied the Japanese language via a satellite program at her high school and had been accepted to attend school in western Japan via the AFS program. So I greeted the students I knew and began to help the city officers write citations to the students for underage drinking.

I suddenly received another Dispatch call for an accident that had occurred near the location of the bar I had been monitoring. I excused myself and rushed to my patrol unit to hurry to the site. I saw the faces of the students as I left and saw their expressions change from unconcerned to ones of wonderment for the call I had just received. I believe it helped sober them up a bit when they saw that something serious had happened.

I notified Dispatch that I was on my way code 3 (lights and siren) to the exact location they were relaying to me.

I visualized the location in my mind and knew it was only two miles away from that bar down a side road. This was one of those times in a Deputy's job when adrenaline flows and heightened awareness comes into play as the patrol unit speeds toward an emergency. This time, the few cars on the road yielded to my lights and siren as I moved closer to the accident scene.

I pondered on what I would discover at the end of my hurried pace: multiple victims, horrible injuries, even death. As I approached the bar I was monitoring, I noticed that the pickup truck of my earlier intention was no longer there. I suddenly knew that he was involved in the accident, intuition probably. I turned at the intersection of the side road and sped toward the accident location, a couple of miles farther, and immediately saw a vehicle overturned in the ditch at the first sharp curve. I notified Dispatch that I was on scene, killed my siren but left my lights flashing to warn other traffic and illuminated the accident scene with my headlights and spotlight. I exited my vehicle and immediately noticed a body on top of the overturned pickup, which I recognized as the one I had been watching.

I had to climb onto the pickup in order to check the status of the man who was not badly injured or disfigured. A pulse check on his neck told me that he was dead, probably from a broken neck as he exited the vehicle the hard way: through the windshield. He had evidently failed to notice or make the curve and rolled the pickup. I could only shake my head in sadness for the guy whom I probably could have saved had it not been for being called away on the student party backup. *What a waste,* I thought. He was a man in his middle age and literally drank his life away. I sermonize on this a bit because it was our job to try and prevent such tragedies and in this case, the circumstances dictated that that was not to be. This calamity has forever been indelibly etched into my memories.

I immediately informed Dispatch via my handheld radio of what I found and requested they notify the coroner and an ISP officer. Almost always an Idaho State Patrol was needed for a fatal accident. That was their specialty: accident reconstruction.

Perhaps a half hour later I saw the ISP squad car approach and saw that it was my friend, Tim, whom I worked with regularly. I brought him up to speed on what happened, including my missed chance of saving the man, and we immediately began the long process of accident reconstruction. The camera work was first detailing the whole scene and then skid marks to measure the probable speed of the vehicle. We used an apparatus that we dragged along the road to determine a coefficient of friction. That, along with distance measurements, gave us a pretty good idea of the speed at which the vehicle was traveling when the accident occurred, the end point.

Without getting too involved in explaining the formulas and means the reconstruction uses, suffice it to say the person's vehicle was traveling at about 45 mph entering a curve the was posted at 25 mph. The dulled senses and reaction of the driver were too little, too late. He simply went through the curve while trying to turn, which caused the pickup to flip. Of course the man was not wearing his seatbelt and more than likely would have survived the crash. The rooftop of the pickup was not badly caved in and I am sure that if he had been wearing his seatbelt, he would have survived without major injury.

Most practiced drunk drivers will put on their seatbelts; not so much for safety but they know they can be stopped for small traffic infractions, which lead to their arrest for DUI. In this case, I'm sure he didn't think it necessary since his home wasn't too far from the accident scene. What can be said other than "would've, could've, should've"?

Our investigation had lasted for about three hours and the sun was beginning to make its appearance. I was already three hours overtime in my shift, the coroner had come and gone, and the body brought to a funeral home for analysis and preparation. Tim told me to go home and that he would wrap things up. I gladly concurred and thanked him for his help. I was exhausted! I informed Dispatch that I would be 10-42 (ending my shift) and heading home.

After shedding my gear and uniform it did not take me long to sleep. My day was done. I never did find out the level of B.A.C. via the toxicology report, but I would bet it was at least double the limit.

Chapter 11
Hunting Drunks

If I was to say what part of the job I preferred, it was going after drunk drivers. I had no compunction in doing what I had to do to find them. They were dangerous and for me the end justified the means. Now, don't get me wrong; that didn't mean anything unethical, immoral, or illegal. It just meant I would use any small or large violation of traffic law to stop vehicles during the "witching hours". As explained before, those hours were between 10 pm and 2 am. It was possible to encounter an inebriated driver outside of those hours, but rarely.

I never sat on bars waiting for people to leave. That was bad business and bad for the businesses. It would be like shooting a bear in a cage. No, no, I was fair and gave them a head start. I'm joking, of course, but many in the public believed we were that cunning and despicable. In reality, all of my drunk arrests were made by simply doing traffic control at night: observing speed, failure to stay in one's lane, and any other erratic driving. Or simple burned-out headlights or tail lights were a good reason to stop a vehicle.

In the previous chapter I related a case where I tried to catch a habitual drunk driver but failed. In my way of looking at it, I was not only trying to protect the general public but also the culprit by making them aware of their bad deeds and trying to keep from killing themselves.

In my time as a Deputy I probably made around fifty such arrests. Each and every one a different story.

One night, I was traveling north to Payette on Highway 55 when I radared a vehicle speeding southbound toward the next small village. I quickly turned my patrol unit and pursued the offender. With overhead lights flashing, I rapidly caught up to the vehicle. However, it did not stop but continued on. I used my siren to also alert the driver, but to no avail. I radioed in my position and the car's license plate and requested a backup unit. I simply didn't know what I had caught, but it felt like a "whale".

Sergeant Joe responded to my backup request and said he would be with me promptly. I responded "10-4." As we approached the small town, the vehicle turned and stopped by the local log cabin bar, a well-known watering hole for locals. I told Dispatch that I had the vehicle stopped and would wait for Sergeant Joe to arrive. Failure to yield to a police unit is a serious violation and situation, which could harbor all kinds of scenarios. I wasn't taking any chances. My backup quickly arrived and we approached the vehicle as if it was a serious event. With guns drawn, we approached the car, which was a larger, newer SUV, with Joe on the passenger side and me the driver's side. The driver had his window down and was protesting the stopping of his car. I told him to keep his hands where I could see them and produce his driver's license and other documents. However, the license wasn't required for me to know who I had stopped. It was the well-known owner of the log cabin bar.

Understanding that it was not as dangerous as we thought, we re-holstered our weapons and proceeded with a likely DUI inquest. It was obvious to us both that the man was drunk and after establishing probable cause to that assumption I had the driver step out of the vehicle. I explained to him that I thought he was over the legal limit of .08 B.A.C. and I wanted to do some sobriety tests on him. He complied and I started first with the Horizontal Gaze Nystagmus test (HGN).

This test, along with an accompanying one, the Vertical Gaze Nystagmus (VGN), involved watching the subject's eyes move. These tests were developed by the medical and scientific community and indicated anomalies in eye movement when a subject's blood alcohol level is elevated. It establishes points for various movements that count up against the inebriated person. I usually only had to do the HGN in order to determine an approximate level of B.A.C. If I wanted to see how much more the individual was intoxicated, I would perform a VGN, which added more points to the result. These tests are well-respected and a proven method of determining probable cause in the arrest of a driver while DUI. Many court decisions have confirmed and upheld them.

I told him to not move his head but to only follow the point of my pen with his eyes as I moved it left to right and back again about twelve inches away. Commonly, people would move their head and I would have to repeat, "Don't move your head; just follow with your eyes." Scientifically, the test had been established with points attributed to poor functioning of the eyes. If the eyes didn't smoothly flow following the object, those were strong negatives. If when the eyes reached the maximum point to one side or the other, they bounced, those were other strong negatives.

There were other subtle indicators that showed excessive alcohol in the blood. The difference in the VGN test was that I would move the pen up and down instead of side to side; it indicates a greater degree of intoxication. Without going into further detail, the HGN test was the best for establishing intoxication. I was never wrong with this test.

Other tests included the walk and turn where one had to walk a straight line nine steps placing each foot in front of the other, heel to toe, and then turning and doing the same thing back. This test was all about balance. Another was the one leg stand where one had to stand on one leg with their hands at their sides. Normally, it's not a difficult exercise unless one has a physical impairment or is drunk. I commonly had drivers recite the alphabet, which in many cases was quite humorous. Most drunks were all over the place with their alphabet recital and I would have to write correctly in my report how they said it. Being that I recorded everything, that was easy but still funny.

I established that my detainee was indeed "drunk" or over limit. I arrested him on the charge of DUI and booked him into the jail. Sergeant Joe later told me he was jealous because he had been trying to get this guy for a while, but also added, "Good job."

Most of my arrests were of men. I would estimate that fully ninety percent of DUI/DWI arrests throughout the country are of male drivers, which makes sense since men are the predominant customers of bars and liquor stores. Women, in my mind, are more sensible. They still consume alcoholic beverages but at home or in moderate amounts outside of the home. This is just my personal opinion based on my experiences as a Deputy and also knowing how my wife, Helena, comports herself. She watches what I drink when we're out in restaurants and will <u>always</u> drive home if feeling that I drank too much. With that in mind, the night that I arrested the only woman in my career was a snowy one.

I was patrolling just outside the same small town where I had made the arrest I just related. I came upon a car that was weaving back and forth across its lane; the snow hadn't accumulated yet and the road lines were clear. Failure to maintain one's lane of travel is a violation, so I made a stop of the offender. Once I had notified Dispatch, I approached the car. With snowflakes falling, I addressed the driver; a middle-aged woman. With slurred speech, she asked why I stopped her. I informed her that she was weaving all over the road and I was concerned about her condition. She said, "I just left the Log Cabin bar and am going home."

With that comment, she was making my job easy. With the smell from the auto, her bad driving, and admission of being at the bar, I told her, "Ma'am, I think you are drunk and want you to exit the car." Whereupon I performed the usual sobriety tests. There was no question in my mind that from the HGN test alone she was well over the limit. So I arrested her, placed her in the back of my car, and called for a tow truck for her vehicle. There wasn't anything exceptional about this DUI arrest other than the fact it involved a woman. It was not a common occurrence with any other Deputy, either.

My last anecdotal story of a DUI arrest perhaps was the most shocking. I was pretty adept at determining a person's level of intoxication until the night I came across the most practiced drunk I ever stopped.

I was traveling north on Warren Wagon Road, which ran alongside the western shore of Lake Payette, when I came upon a vehicle that was driving somewhat slowly. *No big deal*, I thought until the car broke slightly and I saw that one of the brake lights was burned out. So, being it was a fairly quiet night, I decided to stop the vehicle and just warn the driver about the brake light. I informed Dispatch of my position, plate number and make of vehicle.

I, as always, cautiously approached the driver's side and noticed that both front windows were opened, unusual, being it a cold night. I told him the reason for the stop and then began to realize the reason for the open windows. It is common for drunk drivers to do that to clear the car of the smell from someone who had been drinking. However, I still detected some of the odor from alcoholic beverages. I use those words because in our reports we are required to use them instead of "the smell of alcohol," which does not emit any odor.

I asked for his documents and, upon receiving them, I asked, "Have you been drinking tonight?"

He replied, "I have only had a couple." Now, I might add that his speech was not slurred, although slow and correct, nor anything else evident that indicated a DUI. I told him to stay in the vehicle and that I would return shortly.

Now my suspicions were strong that something was not copacetic with the man, so upon returning I asked him to recite the alphabet. He said he would and slowly recited as if having to think about it until he missed "f" in his recital. A normal driver with no alcohol in their system can rattle off the alphabet quickly, but when they have to think and slowly do it, that's a big flag. Most intoxicated drivers know they are guilty and try not to challenge the officer. In this case, he had the perfect right to reject my request and that would have left me with insufficient probable cause to proceed with sobriety tests.

But his mistake opened that door. Again, knowing one's rights is paramount.

I then told him that I thought he was over the limit and ordered him to step out of the car to perform several sobriety tests. When I did those, I usually situated the person between my patrol unit and their car. This provided protection from other traffic and ample light from my headlights.

The HGN in his case showed intoxication but not excessive. He performed the other tests; walk and turn and one legged stand, fairly well. So, I thought I had just another "run of the mill" drunk driver, nothing extreme. So I placed him under arrest, informed Dispatch, and called for a tow truck. After about a half an hour, I brought him to the Mountain County Jail for booking.

Before I turned him over to the jail staff, we went to the testing room. I explained that I would be testing him twice and when he exhaled into the machine tube to blow steadily and continue, I told him to stop. He complied and when the report ticket came out, I was shocked! In my stunned reaction of what I saw, I blurted out, "Das ist unglaublich," German for "That is unbelievable." Based on my observations of his comportment, I knew I had arrested a very practiced drunk.

I simply couldn't believe the reading of .35 B.A.C. coming from this man. Also, some time had already passed since his last drink and his body had burned off some of the alcohol. With the amount of alcohol in his system, he should have been unconscious or even dead. It was hard to accept what the machine was telling me, so, of course, we did the second test, which was the same as the first. It confirmed what I had. I checked the logs of the machine and it had been tested and checked by Bryan, the Deputy certified and responsible for checking the Intoxylizer 4000 machine every day. So, I was sure that the machine was correct.

What was simply astounding, however, was the person was

able to function, even more so at the level he did. He always got away with it; that was incredible!

I booked him into the jail and advised the supervisor of what I had discovered and told him to monitor the man in case he needed medical attention.

Evidently I had done my job well because the Court never called me to be a witness in the case. I only prayed that he didn't eventually kill himself or someone else in his practiced roll as a drunk driver.

I saw my role as a Deputy stopping intoxicated drivers as a "lifeguard" to the general driving public. According to the NHSTA (National Highway Traffic Safety Administration), 11,654 people were killed in drunk driving crashes in 2020 in the U.S.; about 32 individuals each day. And the numbers keep climbing each year. That is absolutely unacceptable when understanding the pain caused by these thoughtless drivers. What is just as bad, in my opinion, are people that are driving and texting. They are even more inattentive than most drunk drivers, since at least a drunk is trying to get home and is focusing more on his driving but is just not able to respond quickly enough to unexpected exigencies. So it was that I pursued this part of my job with gusto.

Chapter 12
The Big Bust

When we were not occupied with other calls, we would gather a few outstanding warrants from Patti's file and go looking for the person named. Now, a warrant is an official document issued by the Court for various reasons. The most common we had was failure to appear. That means that upon release from jail on bond, a person commits to appear in Court on a specific day and time to answer for the charge against them, and later doesn't comply. It really wasn't a difficult process since the document had all of the culprit's information. It was only a matter of catching them. That was the hard part since they were hyper sensitive to any Deputy's approach.

Most of my arrests occurred during traffic stops after Dispatch informed me that the driver or a passenger I checked had an outstanding warrant. One time, I arrested two from the same car, "Birds of a feather flock together." However, the most challenging of all took me some time, investigating, and patience.

Pam had an outstanding warrant for failure to appear on a drug charge and no one was able to catch her. So I decided to do it and began finding out all the information about her that I could. Her daughter lived in one of the small towns and as I passed her house, which was situated on the main highway, I would look for her presence there. I knew she was key to my investigation and one day I saw that a car was parked outside. So I immediately stopped, went to the front door, and visibly surprised her. She said, "What do you want?" I explained that I wanted to "talk" with her mother, Pam, and asked if she knew where she was. She said she had no idea and couldn't give me any information. I knew she was lying but left it at that.

I learned as well that Pam's boyfriend, George, was an Aryan Nation adherent and was known to deal in drugs as well. To those reading who may not know what the Aryan Nation was about, it was a non-homogenous group of anti-law, some would call radical neonazis, who opposed the current way the government was usurping citizens' rights and abusing its power. It was centered in northern Idaho, out of Kootenai County, not far from Mountain County. Adherents were spread throughout Idaho and other states and often shaved their heads, making them known as "Skinheads."

I had obtained the make and plate number of the pickup he drove, which gave me another piece of the puzzle. Little by little, I was making a picture of their lives and how they operated. So my focus was to watch for his vehicle and follow it to the "treasure." I had also located their place of residency; a South Wind motorhome up on a hillside about a quarter of a mile off the Farm to Market roadway. It was completely visible from the road and I made it a point to pass by often and to observe if I could see anyone there.

One day, with my Lieutenant, Richard, accompanying me in my patrol unit, we stopped to scope out the location with binoculars. Richard, while watching the place, saw a person walk around the motorhome and go inside. *Ah-ha*, I thought, *we finally have them.*

I drove up to the home and pointed to a sign that said, "$5000 penalty for any law officer entering this property," an indication we were dealing with a advocate of the Aryan Nation.

We exited the patrol unit and went to the door. I stood back while Richard knocked. No one answered. He knocked again and announced, "Sheriffs's Department," but to no avail. They were just too cunning to open that door. So Lieutenant Richard indicated for us to leave, knowing it would be illegal for us to force entry without a warrant.

We had to be patient. Our opportunity would come.

Over the next couple of weeks, we both patrolled past the location, often looking for that opportunity. One day, I was driving west on a road perpendicular to the Farm to Market with my Reserve Deputy, Tom, who was a frequent rider with me. Suddenly, I saw the pickup for which I was searching coming at us. I almost shouted, "That's him. That's the truck I'm looking for."

I explained to Tom what I meant and told him to get ready

for a fun ride. I waited for the truck to pass over a hill and disappear before I turned. I didn't want to alert George, the boyfriend, that I was turning on him. As we approached at a distance. I wanted to find a reason to stop him; any kind of traffic violation. We continued to follow and waited.

Sure enough, when George paused at the stop sign at the intersection of Farm to Market, he failed to signal right. I exclaimed, "We've got him."

I sped up to the intersection and turned right to follow and when I was close, I turned on my overhead lights. Well, he decided to ignore them and continued driving toward his home. I used the siren several times and he simply put his arm out the window and waved me to go around. I looked at Tom and said, "What an idiot!" I immediately called for backup, telling them the vehicle I was following, the location, and its refusal to stop. I immediately heard from Lance, a Payette City officer, that he was responding code 3.

We continued on for another mile, where at his driveway he turned and stopped. I radioed Dispatch that he had stopped at that location and we would be involved in a felony takedown. Knowing that this "hombre" carried weapons, I was taking no chances. I told Tom to grab the shotgun and stand at his door frame with the gun pointed at the driver's side. I as well stood by my door frame with my pistol aimed at the vehicle. I then began my instructions according to our training for dangerous arrests. With the microphone in hand, I told him to turn off his engine.

"Take the keys from the ignition and with both hands

outside your window, drop the keys to the ground. Open the truck door with the outside handle and exit the truck with your back toward me." After he exited the vehicle as per my commands, I continued, "Now walk backwards toward the sound of my voice until I tell you to stop. Now stop and put your hands behind your head with your fingers interlocked."

At that point, I holstered my gun, moved around my car door, and put him against the pickup bed, where I handcuffed him, as all the while Tom maintained vigilance with his shotgun. I then placed him in the back of the patrol unit and radioed Dispatch that we had one in custody.

Lance had just arrived and we discussed what had just happened. He said he would handle the search of the vehicle and impounding.

I called Dispatch again and informed them that we needed a tow truck for the pickup. Of course George, upon hearing me request that, shouted, "Wait, don't do that. My girlfriend is up at the house and she can drive it."

I turned around and said, "Oh, is Pam there?"

He immediately realized his mistake and clammed up. I knew then I had two arrests that day. I stepped out of my patrol unit with Tom and we had a pow wow with Lance. I informed them that we would proceed up to George's "home", such as it was, and arrest Pam on her outstanding warrant. We would surround the motorhome and make sure there were no avenues of escape.

Both patrol units approached the house and we exited to execute my plan. Lance was on the opposite side. looking in through a window, and as I knocked, I heard him shout, "What are you doing in there?" Shortly after my second, harder knock on the door, a skinny, haggard-looking woman opened the door and asked what we wanted. I asked her, "Are you Pam?" to which she replied yes.

She was casually eating a bowl of ice cream and I noticed a small male child sitting at the table doing the same. I asked her to step outside to answer some questions, which she did. By then Lance had come around from the other side and asked if I needed help. I held him off for a moment while I informed Pam that I was placing her under arrest for the outstanding warrant. I handcuffed her and told Lance to go ahead with a cursory search. I asked Pam who the boy was and she said it was her grandson. She gave me the daughter's number so I could have her pick up the boy.

Lance immediately informed me that he was finding drug paraphernalia and other illegal items out in the open. By law and court decisions, we are allowed to execute a cursory search of the location for officer safety, in regards to weapons and other plain-view evidence.

When he told me that, I said, "Lance, stop and back out. Bring the boy out and secure the premises. We need to get a search warrant." I knew that if we continued, whatever we found could be thrown out by the court under the "Fruit of the Poisonous Tree" doctrine; which, as I've already mentioned, basically states that any evidence of a crime discovered without a warrant would be rejected by the

Court. He complied and we waited for the mother to pick up the boy.

When she arrived, I chastised her for leaving the boy in such an environment and also for being disingenuous with me before. Needless to say, she was not contrite in the least.

I asked Lance to take Pam in his car since it would not be good to have them both in mine. I informed Dispatch that we needed another unit or detective to secure the location until a warrant was obtained. In the meantime I left Tom on scene to maintain the chain of custody. If I had left the scene without supervision, the defendants' lawyer/s could claim that someone else planted the paraphernalia, drugs, or whatever while the place was unattended. It was mandatory to maintain a clear chain of custody for the Court to demonstrate that no outside intrusion occurred.

Again, I wanted no tainted evidence which could lead to it being exclusionary in the Court proceedings.

Even though I was not officially a detective, I was one in the sense that I had to know the correct methods and requirements for any investigation. We were trained to know and do everything. Our job encompassed all aspects of law enforcement. Our Sheriff depended on us to perform correctly. In this case, I know I did because I was never called to Court as a witness or to testify. As well, report-writing is critical. A Deputy has to write succinctly and properly on "who, what, where, when, how, and why" so the County Attorney understands exactly what happened and then presents it to the Court. Good writing is a skill that is needed but few had.

But that is not the whole story, the hilarious part follows.

After booking in both parties, George on failure to yield and Pam on her outstanding warrant for failure to appear, I immediately went to work on writing my report for the Judge to issue a warrant to search the motorhome. Upon receiving it, I gave it to Pat, the lead Detective, who took the case from there.

I didn't hear for several days regarding the result of the investigation, until I spoke with Sergeant Bill on the side of a back road about the case.

I asked him about it and he exclaimed, "You mean you haven't heard?"

I replied, "No, what did they find?"

He related a story that had me almost rolling in the street with laughter. I couldn't believe what I heard. He said that Pat and K9 Deputy Kimber went into the motorhome to search and let the dog go searching for drugs. The dog went directly to the small bathroom and hit on the toilet just inside the door. Kimber opened the toilet seat, the dog sniffed inside it and immediately ran out the door and started puking. Kimber as well got a hearty whiff of the smell and followed the dog and vomited as well.

I couldn't believe what I was hearing.

Pat, after witnessing this calamity was more circumspect in his examination of the toilet but still succumbed to the odor and followed suit. I was laughing so hard upon Bill's telling of the story that I could hardly contain myself.

Why did the dog hit on the toilet, and what was in it?

According to Bill, it was full to the top with shit and on top of the mess was a lot of white, powdered methamphetamine. The dog had detected it but when it got close to the rank smell of decaying feces, the poor thing was overwhelmed.

Undeterred after recovering himself, Pat said he was going back in to recover the evidence. Using a spoon from the kitchen, he scooped the white powder from the surface of the crap and put it in an evidence bag. It was enough to seal the conviction.

So after hearing this account of what happened, I understood what Lance had seen before, when he shouted, "What are you doing in there?" Pam had rushed to the bathroom to dump a bag of methamphetamine on the full-to-the-brim "colonic waste". She figured that would be enough to hide a felonious act. Wrong! The sensitivity of a drug dog's sense of smell is incredible and hard to fool.

No doubt it was a very funny ending and it was the icing on the cake for me.

Although the Sheriff never said a word to me about the case, no congratulations, no thank you, I was still proud of what I had accomplished. I brought two deserving people to justice and eliminated one source of drugs that was on the street.

When one sees the horrible effects that methamphetamines have on the human body, it's hideous. It changes the beautiful complexion of a person into one of ugliness: red blotches, scarring, and a haggard look. It destroys the body. Cocaine, although similar in its high, isn't nearly as destructive as the powerful chemical concoction that is meth. Because it was so cheap to buy it was the second most prevalent drug found during searches behind marijuana; it was becoming an epidemic and I was pleased to intercept one source. However I felt it was a losing battle. In this case, my patience and perseverance paid off. It was my biggest bust, which made the job worthwhile.

The end of the case was that George went to prison for a while on a drug distribution charge, and was released on parole. Pam was given some jail time in Buffalo with parole.

Sometimes what one finds out during an arrest can be simply astounding. Such was the case with a group of hunters in the backwoods of the Payette National Forest. It was hunting season and a Federal Forest Officer, Dave, requested my help in investigating a shooting at a camp after sunset. He had received a report from a Federal Forest worker, not an LEO, of a disturbance in a hunting zone along the Little Salmon River.

So, around 8 pm we headed out in our two patrol units. It was October, when the daylight hours were diminishing and darkness came around 6 pm. Upon arriving at the campsite, there was a big fire blazing in the fire pit with a group of about six hunters drinking and arguing. When we showed up, one hunter approached us and said one of the other guys tried to shoot him.

They, of course, had been drinking and arguing about something stupid and it had gotten out of control. The aggressor had said he was going to shoot the complainant. They had both picked up their rifles, which were still loaded and fired at each other. The victim missed his shot but the threatening hunter incredibly hit the receiver part of the victim's rifle positioned at his midsection. That rifle was destroyed by the shot, but it saved the man's life. Others of the party disarmed them both before someone was hurt or killed.

Dave and I looked at each other and couldn't believe what we were hearing and seeing. Although it was a group of friends who were together at the camp, not all the friends were "friends." Two groups of them were not necessarily well-known by the others; so ensued disagreements after much alcohol consumption. One thing led to another, which suddenly became dangerous and explosive.

After sorting out as best as we could what had happened, I decided to arrest both involved in the shootout. I figured it was better to let the County Attorney and the Court decide who was culpable and who was innocent. We confiscated both weapons and upon examination of the damaged rifle, both Dave and I could only shake our heads at how lucky the one hunter was. The bullet had destroyed the receiver mechanism and rendered it totally inoperative.

Being only two LEOs out in the wilderness with a group of drunk hunters was ripe for disaster. Fortunately, we kept our cool and calmed it all down. By his authority, Dave instructed the group to break camp and leave the next morning. They were banned from hunting in the Payette National Forest for the rest of the year.

This all illustrates how the Sheriff and his Deputies have preeminence in enforcing law even on Federal lands. Dave knew that he was probably not facing something he could charge under Federal law; it was a state law issue. We worked together in handling the case.

Chapter 13
Deputy on Horseback

Throughout western U.S. history and culture, the Deputy Sheriff on horseback was well-known and well-respected. The Sheriff and his Deputies were vital in maintaining law and order in their counties, and this was accomplished for many decades on horseback. Most modern-day Sheriff's Departments have some sort of a Posse Patrol arm for use in either search and rescue or going into areas where motorized vehicles can't or aren't permitted to access.

That was the case for the Mountain County Sheriff's Department, as well.

In the rural areas of Idaho, most youths learned to ride horseback at an early age. Tony, our Sheriff, liked riding his horse and was always looking for an excuse to use it for an official reason.

That came about one day when he received a warrant for a man working in the Frank Church River of No Return

Wilderness Area. This area was partially located in Mountain County and is the largest contiguous wilderness in the lower 48 states, with almost 2.4 million acres. It is very much a wilderness region, with tall mountains and deep canyons, one deeper than the Grand Canyon. The suspect was working at a private ranch within the Wilderness, which meant getting him was by horseback only.

Knowing that I also owned horses, he asked me to assist in the capture and arrest of the man. What the warrant on the man was about, I cannot recall, only that he was a wanted man. Todd, another Deputy, was also another horseman but didn't have a horse. Since I had four, Tawnee, a buckskin, Cheyenne, a sorrel, Tyrone, a big bay, and Shoshone, my young, inexperienced part-sorrel, part-palomino, I let Todd use Tyrone.

Now, Tyrone was a 17-hand ex rodeo horse that was nearly 20-years-old, but when kicked into high gear, he could outrun almost everything. He was tame and dependable to the point where children could play around his legs and he wouldn't move at all. I could put any beginner on him and not be the least concerned for their safety. So with Todd on his back, and Todd being tall, they made a perfect team.

I used my favorite horse, Tawnee. She was younger than Tyrone, but with a lot of cattle experience. I had used her in Wyoming, helping on cattle drives, one which was with Oprah Winfrey and her boyfriend, Stedman Graham. It was a fall cattle drive bringing down cattle from the summer range for a rich Chicago banker in the Bighorn Mountains near Sheridan. But that's another story.

The three of us gathered at the Sheriff's house and planned our entry into the Wilderness area and how to find and arrest the man. The date and time were decided along with what we generally needed to pack on the horses.

Now, this ranch was established long before the River of No Return Wilderness was enacted by Congress in 1980, and had its own airstrip. Although no motorized nor mechanical vehicles, including bicycles, were allowed, the preexisting airstrips were allowed to operate under a grandfather clause. I guess Congress incorporated that stipulation in the act to avoid having to spend millions of dollars more to buy out all the existing private properties inside the Wilderness zone. This ranch utilized several air services out of the Payette City Airport. So if we arrested the man, it was agreed that Todd would fly the prisoner out.

With our plan formed, the day arrived. Sheriff Tony had his own horse trailer for his horse and I had my double trailer to haul my two horses. After fully packing and preparing, we headed out in the afternoon. We drove toward Yellow Pine, an isolated village near the Wilderness area. At the end of the road, we reached a campsite where we set up camp. The plan was to start on the trail leading to the ranch early in the morning so as to arrive as early as possible and execute our arrest plan. We did not want to alert the individual we were seeking. We also needed sufficient time to fly him out and to return back to the campsite, so we left at sunrise.

I felt like I was in a western movie as we headed out. Sheriff Tony led the way according to a detailed map of the trails leading to the ranch. We did not push the horses but proceeded at a steady walking pace. I marveled at the beauty of the forest, sounds of the wildlife, and occasional spotting of wild animals. It was definitely a wilderness wonderland in which I delighted. We didn't converse much since we were riding single-file, and only occasionally stopped to consult on the proper path to take. The weather was perfect this late June day, with bright blue skies, a slight breeze, and moderate temperatures.

So, as we approached the ranch hidden in the forest, we quickly settled on a reconnoiter place to scope out the lay of the buildings and open areas. We tied the horses in a grassy area to a rope strung between two trees, and with binoculars we went to the forest edge to try to see anyone moving about. Being that it was only seven in the morning, we didn't see much activity.

It was eventually decided that Todd would walk in, surreptitiously, and locate the person. At that moment, he would only locate him and by radio tell us where to meet.

The Sheriff took up position near the main ranch house and I near the horses at the opposite end. Our objective was to prevent the man from escaping if he got wind of us.

Suddenly, it was all over. Todd called us and told us he located him in a barn, working, and had arrested him.

Wow, that was no fun. I wanted some action. But like most such events, it turned out to be anticlimactic. We did our jobs right. Darn, no bloodshed or gunfight. My illusion was shattered!

I say that "tongue in cheek," of course, because really no sensible western Deputy wants that. I don't know about those eastern ones though, they can be bloodthirsty. Ha, only kidding.

We called the air service to fly in to the airstrip to transport Deputy Todd and his prisoner back to Payette, where a patrol Deputy was waiting to bring Todd and the man back to Buffalo to book into the jail. After we saw the plane off, the Sheriff and I began our return trek back to the campsite.

We proceeded at a faster pace, with me handling two horses.

At times I outpaced Tony and he grumbled that I was going too fast. I thought, *Too bad, buck it up and be a real horseman.* When we got to the trailers I noticed that he was quiet and a little grumpy, since I think he was pissed that I out performed him on horseback. Our relationship declined after that until the day he resigned his office. He was a pretty vain man who really wasn't suited for the job.

With the coming of the Fourth of July celebrations that year, the Sheriff scheduled us to participate in the Buffalo parade on horseback. This hadn't happened for years, but Sheriff Tony wanted to display his team on horseback as well as in patrol cars, boats, and snowmobiles used by the department. I figured *Why not? It should be fun.* So I cleaned up Tawnee and Tyrone, my saddle, scabbard, saddle bags, and rope to really look the part. The parade crowd loved us and it put a real shine on our image.

Tawnee was a very pretty buckskin mare who the crowd

loved. She handled the raucous nature of the parade well, with people coming close to take pictures. Although in the group of horses I owned, she was low on the "totem pole," by herself she shined. She never once pushed her ears back in annoyance, but was ever watchful and prepared to react if something went wrong. I was proud of her and I told her so.

Horses know and understand kindness and love from their masters.

Now, Tyrone, on whom was Todd again, was just the opposite. He was so placid and unfazed that I don't think anything would have surprised him. He was so used to crowds and noise at rodeos that a simple parade was "kinderspiel"–kids play.

All in all, the parade was a success and very enjoyable for us all. I think it put the Sheriff's Department in a good light, and that was what we were all about; creating goodwill to the people of Mountain County.

Chapter 14
Investigation

As a Law Enforcement Officer, I was trained to do everything including investigations, which were mostly handled by our department Detectives.

One day, as I was sitting in the front office talking with Patti and Connie, a couple in their middle ages came in seeking help with a credit card problem. They explained that they had just returned to their home south of Buffalo after spending the winter in Arizona, and had received a credit card bill in their names with an outstanding balance of around two thousand dollars. They told me they did not recognize this particular credit card nor the charges. All were charges made during the previous December, when they were living in Arizona. They confirmed that they never opened this account with this particular credit card company. They felt a fraud had occurred and needed our help.

I got all of their information, including their home address, driver's licenses, social security numbers, and telephone numbers. I then asked them about their house and if they closed it down while away or if someone cared for it in their absence. They told me that a younger woman who was related to friends of theirs stayed at the home during their time in Arizona and had access to their mail.

My instinct immediately told me that I had my suspect, and I proceeded along that thread. They gave me all her information and family contacts. I assured them that I would pursue the matter diligently and would contact them if I needed more information or help. To quote a famous detective, "The game was afoot."

It was quite apparent to me that the caretaker was able to acquire enough personal information, mainly social security numbers, to open a credit card account and use it to the max. Most new credit card offerings were for a maximum of two thousand dollars. Upon examination of the numerous charges on the account, most were under one hundred dollars, which made them misdemeanor charges, but the ones over that amount were felonies. Also, just fraudulently opening a credit card account is a felony. In total there were about ten felony crimes and numerous misdemeanor ones associated with this account. I had my work cut out for me.

I began by calling the credit card company based in Salt Lake City.

After explaining to the several operators who I was and what I wanted, I finally got to the right department.

A person in the Fraud Department asked me what I was

calling about. I said, "I am Deputy Alfred Anderson, with the Mountain County Sheriff's and am investigating a fraudulent credit card account." I gave her all the account information, which she then opened on her computer. I began with my many questions like: when was it opened, what was the social security number associated, an itemized ledger of charges and locations and signatures.

She told me that before any private information could be released, she would need an official document from and signed by the Sheriff requesting the information. I told her I would do that after getting her office contact information. The long investigative process began. All correspondence was via the mail.

I spoke with Sheriff Tony about it and he had Patti draft a letter, which he signed. It went out immediately. In the meantime, I began making calls.

I first went to the home of the complainants to get a perspective of the house and its location. I further questioned them about where they kept their sensitive documents and who handled their mail.

From that point, I had enough information to make a call to the caretaker's mother. I didn't make any overt charges or claims to anyone I spoke to, only that I was wanting to talk to Mary, the caretaker, about a private matter. I asked the mother where her daughter was living and how I could contact her. Of course the mother was very concerned why a Deputy was looking for her and what it was about. I kept it all low-key so as to not alert Mary that I was conducting a criminal investigation. All the mother would tell me was that her daughter was down in Boise, working part-time for a company. She did give me the name of the company and so the thread led there.

Days later, I was given permission by the Sheriff to further investigate and go down to Boise. I had located the business for which Mary supposedly worked and went down in my patrol car in plain clothes to talk with someone there. I met with the owner of the company, explained who I was, showed him my credentials, and began to inquire about Mary. He was instantly reticent to tell me anything and wanted to know what I was investigating her for. I told him I couldn't divulge that and that I only wanted to speak to her about a private matter.

He said, "Well, I don't think I can tell you anything, then."

I told him that officially I could have him subpoenaed but would rather avoid the hassle. I only wanted to know if he knew her, if she had worked for him, and where I might contact her.

After realizing I was serious, he admitted that she had worked there but no longer. That all he knew was she was living in Puyallup, Washington, but didn't know exactly where. I thanked him and returned back to Mountain County with another lead to follow.

The next day, I called the Pierce County Sheriff's Department and got a hold of a Detective. I explained who I was and that I needed help in locating Mary. I gave him all the info I had on her and he said he would try to find her. I asked as well for help if I needed to go over and arrest her and he assured me that it would be no problem.

It all came to a head one evening while I was sitting in the Dispatch room talking to the Dispatchers. Suddenly, their phone rang and Vic told me that Mary was calling looking for me. I guess the heat was on and she wanted to talk.

I answered the phone and said, "Deputy Anderson, to whom am I speaking?" She said her name and asked why I was looking for her. I replied obliquely, "Look, I am investigating a matter that you might know something about. I would like your help." Again, I was trying to be a real salesman and not spook her. I said that I could meet her there in Puyallup if necessary, but she said she was coming to Buffalo in a few days to meet with her mother and would come to the Sheriff's office. I told her that would be great and asked what day she was coming.

With the meeting set, I hung up and shouted "yahoo!"

Of course the girls wanted to know what was going on and I told them the story. I said, "I can't believe she is going to come in voluntarily and make this easy." After a month of work, I was hopeful it was coming to fruition. The Dispatchers were surprised as well that she was willingly coming to see me. I guess the pressure I was applying was pricking her conscience.

Mary arrived in the morning at the front office and asked to see me. I was back in the Patrol Deputies' room, planning my approach on how to get an admission from her. I was called and went to the front office to greet her. I told her that

I was glad she came in to assist me in my investigation and led her to a separate interrogation room. I was surprised by how young she looked; I guess I shouldn't have been since I knew she was only twenty-two.

I had her sit down and tried to make her feel a little at ease. She was tense and nervous and probably knew what was coming. I explained that I was really investigating her for illegal use of a credit card and needed to read her her rights. The room had a tape recorder, which I had turned on as soon as we entered.

After reading and explaining her rights, she agreed to answer my questions. At this point, she had begun to cry and I put a box of tissues by her to use. I tried to comfort her by not being harsh.

By this time, I had received from the credit card company all the documents I requested, which included all the charges and locations, plus any signatures. Some charges were made at gas pumps which didn't require signatures.

I began by asking her, "Did you apply for a credit card under the victim couple's names?"

She replied, "Yes." Felony number one admission.

I then proceeded down the list of all the charges on the credit card statement and asked her if she was the person who made the charges. She replied yes to all my questions.

By the end, she had admitted to ten felonies and a number of misdemeanors. I finally asked her why she did it. She tearfully replied that it was Christmas time, she had no money, and wanted to give gifts to her family and friends. She had found the couple's social security numbers and opened one of many credit card offerings that came through the mail. She filled out the form with her forged signature of the husband and shortly thereafter the new cards came in the mail. She went on a spending spree and maxed out the card at two thousand dollars.

I thought, *How did she think she was going to get away with this?*

I tried to calm her down a bit but told her I was placing her under arrest for the crimes. I brought her back to the jail and the staff booked her in. I imagine that she knew she was caught and came back to Buffalo to commiserate with her mother and face the music.

I never had to go to Court on this case. I guess I did my job well. I'm sure the County Attorney worked a plea bargain to avoid jail time for her with the requirement to pay all the charges on the credit card. In my way of thinking, that was probably a sensible resolution to the case. No use in totally destroying a young girl's life, especially after she voluntarily submitted herself to the court.

I will say that my diligence in investigating the case paid off. The couple who brought it to me were very happy it was solved, but also sad for Mary. They learned a very valuable lesson in protecting their private information, especially their social security numbers.

I remember when we used to print them on our personal checks. Boy, how times have changed.

Chapter 15
All Good Things End

As I said earlier, I had seen the "handwriting on the wall." Two reasons forced me to resign my position and career as a Deputy. I had immensely enjoyed my time as a Deputy for the Mountain County Sheriff; I consider it my favorite job. Even though the pay sucked, it didn't matter to me. I was fully able to provide for myself and my daughter without concern.

Like a busy tree rodent, I was able to squirrel away enough nuts to last my life.

That was the thing, though I already had things. I had no debt, I owned my house and cars, and decided to call it quits. It was far too risky to continue this occupation and compromise it all. One lawsuit would devastate us and I was not prepared to let that happen. So I "cashed in my chips" and started on a more secure path.

My daughter was also desirous to pursue a university education in the Japanese language. For me, it seemed a logical choice being that Japan was still a predominant world economy with many Japanese businesses and businessmen entering the western U.S.

So she chose the University of Oregon in Eugene as the school to attend since it had a majors program in Japanese and East Asian studies, which she obtained both. The problem was that the out of state tuition was very expensive. I simply couldn't afford it.

And so, "westward ho" we went. She went on to Eugene to start the new school year while I began the process of selling our homestead; which was ten acres, a house, and barn that I built for our horses nestled up against the Payette National Forest. I hated to sell it because we would be leaving great friends and neighbors behind, as well as a beautiful forest to walk in, ride in with our four-wheeler, and hunt elk. It was a paradise. Shortly before this, I had sold all of my horses, Tawnee, Tyrone, Shoshone, and Cheyenne. We weren't riding them much and it wasn't right to just pasture them and let them grow fat. They needed to be worked. My cowboy days were over. A story for another time.

After finding and buying a nice house in the country a couple miles south of Eugene, I made the move, with great sadness. I returned to my home near Payette to complete the signing of papers and pack up my remaining items.

That morning, around 7:30 am mountain time, I was in bed watching television when I saw the attack on the Twin Towers. I sat bolt upright when I saw the second plane hit.

Like with the assassination of President Kennedy, everyone remembers where they were. This is one of those times. I'll never forget it.

That was sadness number one. The second, of course, was the realization that I would never return to this beloved home. When one takes an empty piece of land and creates something beautiful and comfortable, it is hard to leave. So I left my home and job, which I loved so much, and moved on.

I will never forget.